The Last
Great Secret
of the
Third Reich

The Last
Great Secret
of the
Third Reich

by

Arthur O. Naujoks

and

Lee Nelson

Council Press
Springville, Utah

ISBN: 1-55517-551-1
v.2

Published by Council Press
Imprint of Cedar Fort Inc.
925 N. Main Springville, Utah, 84663
www.cedarfort.com

Distributed by:

COUNCIL·PRESS™

Typeset by Virginia Reeder
Cover design by Adam Ford
Cover design © 2001 by Lyle Mortimer

Printed in the United States of America
10 9 8 7 6 5 4 3 2 1

Printed on acid-free paper

Library of Congress Control Number: 2001096781

iv

Acknowledgments

It took ten years of patient research on both sides of the Atlantic to gather the building blocks for this story.

Much of the material from U.S. sources was classified after World War II, and was not available for research until the Freedom of Information Act was passed in 1990.

We relied heavily on written interrogation reports with the officers, scientists and civilians surrendering with the U-234 German submarine on May 14, 1945.

When we contacted the Bundesarchiv (German military archives) in Freiburg, Germany, asking for information on the cruise of the U-234 in the Spring of 1945, they said they did not have any U-boat information after January, 1945. The U.S. Library of Congress and the offices of the U.S. Navy Department were much more helpful, as were American newspapers including The Manchester Union, Boston Sunday Post, Boston Post, Boston Daily Globe, Boston Evening Globe, Portsmouth Herald, Boston Herald, and The New York Times. Also helpful were the Burda-Verlag and Bunte Magazine in Germany.

Most of all we thank Professor Dr. Manfred von Ardenne. Following World War II, he and a hundred German scientists were deported to Russia to develop rockets and nuclear weapons. When the Soviet Union collapsed we found him working at a cancer research facility in Dresden, Saxony. He has been most helpful in shedding light on atomic research activities in Germany during the war, and the sabotage effort by German scientists to prevent Hitler from having the first atomic bomb.

A special thanks is due Dr. Gary Sandquist, director of nuclear engineering at the University of Utah, who helped guide us through the technical maze surrounding the history of nuclear arms development, as well as the scientific terms and principles involved. With practically the whole world believing

Germany and Japan were in the stone age of nuclear weapons development during World War II, we could not have argued a contrary case without the help of scientists like Dr. Sandquist.

The Senatsverwaltung-Berlin, Germany, was most helpful in providing information concerning the flooding of the U-Bahn tunnels in Berlin in the spring of 1945.

Dick Sherwood flew B-29 photographic flights over Hiroshima and Nagasaki immediately following the nuclear bomb explosions, and willingly shared these experiences.

The German war diaries recorded on numerous U-boats are detailed and enlightening about submarine warfare in general, but provided very little information about the secret mission of the U-234.

Today, historians in Japan don't seem to be aware that four months before the Hiroshima bombing, a German submarine was heading in their direction, complements of Adolf Hitler, with enough materials and supplies, including plans and scientists, to produce a dozen nuclear bombs.

We don't claim to have all the information concerning the mission of the U-234, or why its captain decided to disobey orders and help the Americans. Nor do we know the full extent to which the Americans utilized the nuclear weapons payload of the U-234, but we think we have enough facts and documents to support what at first might appear to be outrageous claims. Hopefully other researchers will be sufficiently motivated by our story and research to roll up their sleeves and dig more deeply.

Arthur O. Naujoks and Lee Nelson

Introduction

In 1995, on the fiftieth anniversary marking the end of World War II, an unusual visitor stepped onto my doorstep in Salt Lake City. He introduced himself as Dick Sherwood. He said he had heard that I was writing a book about the first atomic bomb.

I invited him in. He explained that he was captain and pilot of a B-29 Super Fortress Bomber, and that Japanese officials had asked him to participate in some gatherings commemorating August 6, 1945, when the atom bomb was dropped on Hiroshima.

He told me his mission that summer morning in 1945 was to take his B-29 down to 200 feet over Hiroshima to photograph the damage, starting with the chaos and fleeing people outside the circle of fire, but also the horror inside the circle.

"If the rest of the world could see what we saw, we would have a different world today," he explained. "The human destruction we witnessed will never be shown to the public."

At one time Dick and I were foes during World War II. Now, Dick and I were in Salt Lake City, sharing our thoughts and experiences about the war as if they had happened yesterday, but our wrinkled faces and graying hair were testaments to the many years which had passed.

"Through all the years," he continued, "I've had to stay busy with my work to keep my mind from reflecting on the utter human waste and chaos we photographed."

He said when pilots wondered why it was necessary to drop a second bomb on Nagasaki, they were told General Groves wanted to test a different kind of fuse—a proximity fuse—and see if there was any advantage to setting off the bomb at a different elevation.

Dick showed me an old picture of him surrounded by his crew. He was silent for a moment, recalling some of the memories.

I related some of my experiences on the Russian front. I explained how we used teams of horses to drag heavy artillery pieces across the frozen ground.

Then I began showing Dick the research I was doing for my book, consisting of newspaper articles, interrogation reports, entries in military log books, telegrams, letters, and even some *Top Secret* military documents.

Like pieces of a puzzle, the documents painted a simple but astonishing picture. Not only did Adolf Hitler intend to flee from his crumbling Third Reich, along with a huge stash of treasure or war booty, but he also made elaborate plans for revenge on the Allies by helping Japan to be the first country to use the atomic bomb.

But Hitler's last desperate attempt to change the outcome of the war was spoiled by the inadvertent actions of Johann Heinrich Fehler, a submarine captain in the German Navy who defied the orders of his Nazi leaders, taking an action that possibly changed the course of modern history. Following is his story.

Chapter 1

At 11 a.m., Saturday, May 19, 1945, the largest submarine most Americans had ever seen—a full 270 feet long—was moving slowly into the harbor at Portsmouth, New Hampshire. The war in Europe had ended ten days earlier, and this was the fourth German submarine to surrender to United States authorities and enter the Portsmouth harbor in the past week.

But there was something different about this giant sub, called the U-234. As it came into port, it was accompanied by an unprecedented fleet of three U.S. destroyers. And while it was carefully guarded far out in the water, nine of its officers and passengers were removed and rushed to shore on the Coast Guard cutter Argo.

As the cutter approached the dock, a wide alleyway was roped off by Marine guards, to allow prisoners a clear passageway to the waiting busses. Reporters and spectators were warned that if they breached the roped-off passageway, they risked being shot! Marine guards, their backs to the prisoners—pointed their rifles in the direction of the crowd. Reporters were told they could not speak with or interview any of the prisoners, nor would they be allowed to board the submarine.

Such forceful security measures caught everyone by surprise. Other surrendering submarines had not been treated in this manner. Three days earlier, the German crew from the U-873, had been marched in handcuffs through the streets of Boston, where they were pelted with insults and garbage. Later that night, in his cell, Kapitanleutnant (lieutenant commander) Fritz Steinhoff of the U-873, broke in half one of the lenses from his eyeglasses and cut an artery in his arm. He died a few hours later at Massachusetts General Hospital.

With the war in Europe finally over, U.S. Naval officers apparently felt it was all right to celebrate with the rest of the country. As the men began to let off steam, German soldiers and sailors had become justified targets of abuse—at least the government had allowed such abuse to occur—until this giant U-234 sub coasted into Portsmouth Harbor.

The bewildered reporters might have pressed harder to get answers to their questions had they known a Navy bomber was waiting at a nearby runway to fly the unnamed prisoners and cargo boxes to Washington D.C.

When the nine prisoners stepped off the Argo onto the walkway, it was obvious to both reporters and spectators that these men were no ordinary members of a submarine crew.

First in line was Major General Ulrich Kessler, commander of the German Luftwaffe (air force) in the Atlantic, an impressive-looking officer in a gray leather trench coat, his cap high in front, and a Knight's Cross tied with a ribbon around his neck. He was proud and strong, looking exactly like Hollywood would portray German military officers for the next fifty years.

Following Kessler was an odd assortment of military and civilian personnel, which to some of the press looked more like hardware salesmen and store clerks than elite German scientists and weapons experts. The names of the civilians were Heinz Schlicke, Franz Ruf, and August Bringenwald. Ruf carried a huge cardboard suitcase.

But the prisoner with the most remarkable demeanor and appearance was Kapitanleutnant Johann Heinrich Fehler, skipper of the giant sub, a man of medium height with lean, intense features, including an eagle nose, fierce blue eyes, slightly receding hairline, and brown hair. He was thirty four years old. The Boston Sunday Post reported that "...tears of anger and humiliation sparkled in the German's eyes as he clumped toward the bus waiting to take him to the Portsmouth Naval Prison!"

Upon leaving the Argo, Fehler protested to Lt. Charles Winslow, commander of the Coast Guard vessel, about the treatment the submarine captain and the other prisoners had received while held at gunpoint, arms folded across their chests. The German submarine commander objected to being treated like a "gangster."

"But that is exactly what you are," the American skipper responded. "Get the Hell off this boat."

Fehler "clomped" toward the waiting busses, tears in his eyes, disappointed that he and his companions had received such a welcome. Certainly the reporters were wondering about such poor losers—these German sea captains.

The reporters didn't know that Fehler, on his first wartime voyage as first mate on the raider Atlantis, had helped sink twenty-two allied vessels.

Johann Heinrich Fehler was born in the Charlottenburg

area of Berlin. After completing secondary school, he had enlisted in the merchant marine as a deck hand on a sailing vessel. After twenty-seven months in the Baltic Sea, he qualified for his seaman's apprenticeship on ocean freighters, and departed on a two-year voyage to the Far East.

When he returned, he entered the German merchant marine academy, Seefahrtschule, earning his mate's certificate. Shortly afterwards, while attending radio school, he was swayed by aggressive recruiters to join the National Socialist Party, though he did not seem to possess any strong political views at the time.

In 1936 Fehler became an officer cadet in the German Navy. After eight weeks of basic training at Stralsund, he proceeded to Kiel for Marine Artillery School. After nine months at the Kriegsmarine war school, he returned to sea for a six-month voyage around Africa.

Upon returning to Germany, after a brief administrative assignment at Glueckstadt, Fehler was assigned as a watch officer with the Sixth Minesweeping Flotilla. His first command was on the minesweeper M-145 out of Wilhelmshaven when Germany started World War II by invading Poland.

By early 1940 Fehler was serving as mines and explosives officer for the raider Atlantis. The former merchant vessel still looked like a merchant vessel, its big guns and torpedoes carefully disguised.

The Atlantis was one of the most successful raiders in the German Navy, responsible for sinking twenty two allied vessels in a single voyage during 1940 and 1941.

After 655 days at sea, the Atlantis was headed along the west coast of Africa back to port for fuel and supplies with a

German submarine, the U-126, tied alongside. While taking on fuel and supplies, a British Cruiser, the Devonshire, appeared on the horizon. Captain Rogge of the Atlantis sent a radio message, claiming the ship was an American freighter.

Captain Oliver of the British Devonshire was not fooled. He opened fire with his two hundred mm guns.

While the battle raged, the German submarine at the side of the Atlantis submerged. The Atlantis was no match for the big guns, and began to sink. Captain Rogge, now severely wounded, ordered the men to abandon ship. The German sailors swam from pieces of floating debris to rubber rafts as the Atlantis disappeared below the surface of the sea. The Devonshire continued on its way, leaving the German sailors to survive as best they could, or drown in the icy Atlantic waters.

In the midst of the wreckage, it was Johann Fehler who took charge, making sure each survivor had a place in one of the rubber rafts. When the U-126 resurfaced, Fehler supervised the rescue effort, instructing the men to tie the rafts end to end in a line, with the front raft secured to the rear of the sub. And thus the sub, with its long tail of rafts began the journey to the nearest German port on the west coast of France over a thousand miles away.

Whenever an enemy ship was sighted on the horizon, the front raft would cut itself and the line of rafts behind it, free, allowing the U-126 to submerge. The men in the rafts then crouched as low as possible, hoping they would not be seen.

When the train of rafts finally reached a safe port on Christmas Eve, 1941, Captain Fehler received the Iron Cross for overseeing this daring rescue of his fellow sailors. In 1943 Fehler was given command of the U-234, a brand new mine-laying sub, one of the two largest subs ever built by the German

Navy, ninety meters in length.

Johann Heinrich Fehler had been the cream of the German Navy, an officer and Nazi whose loyalty to the Third Reich was not questioned. Now, he was a prisoner of war on United States soil.

The people watching the prisoners as they came on shore had no idea what was lying in the cargo of the sub. They were simply puzzled that the Navy was not allowing either citizens or reporters near the vessel. They did not know that after the U-234 had surrendered at sea to the USS Sutton, the U.S. inspectors made some surprising discoveries. Following the inspectors' immediate radio dispatches to Naval headquarters, the administrators at headquarters had quickly sent a list of cargo items to the Pentagon.

This is what the inspectors found. The remaining crew consisted of nuclear scientists and weapons experts. And the cargo included (1) 560 kilograms of enriched uranium (U235), ready-to-use fodder for nearly a dozen nuclear bombs, (2) two disassembled Messerschmidt turbo jet aircraft, capable of flying at elevations and speeds out of reach of American anti-aircraft guns and aircraft, (3) a crate of infra-red proximity fuses designed to trigger nuclear reactions in bombs at pre-set elevations, and (4) all the plans, instructions and expert personnel needed to utilize the above items. Complete supplies for atomic warfare!

Fehler's original orders had been to take the above cargo to Japan. It was learned later that the Japanese scientists were ready and waiting for help from their German allies. The plan was first to destroy the American fleet assembling off the coast of Japan for a fall invasion, and second, to bring the United

States into submission by bombing some of the large cities on its western shores.

However, instead of following orders to head for Japan, Johann Fehler turned around in the middle of the Atlantic and headed northward with the intent of surrendering to the Americans.

Why? At the time, he knew that Germany was losing the war. And he had been listening to his superior officer, Ulrich Kessler, who was convinced they ought to surrender. Fehler listened to Kessler, although he secretly had a cunning plan of his own.

There is no evidence that Fehler had any idea his ship carried a cargo that could alter the outcome of the war in the Pacific and therefore change the course of modern history. While it was common knowledge among German soldiers and sailors that their government was trying to develop a *Wunderwaffe* (super weapon), no one understood the nature of such a weapon. Fehler did not know that pitchblende was a mineral being extracted from old silver mines in East Germany, and that basic uranium (U 238) was being separated from the pitchblende in kilogram quantities at *Trenrohr* facilities in Stuttgart and Berlin, producing enriched uranium (U-235).

He also didn't know the crate of infrared proximity fuses on his boat were designed to detonate nuclear bombs at pre-set elevations. He didn't know the two disassembled Messerschmidt turbojet aircraft on his sub were capable of delivering two nuclear devices at elevations up to 40,000 feet at speeds exceeding those of American pursuit aircraft. He didn't know the crates of top-secret documents in his hold, and the extra passengers, had all the information and know-how

Japanese scientists needed to begin using nuclear weapons against the Americans. He didn't know Japan had its own nuclear scientists who had been busily digging uranium and experimenting with separation processes, in partnership with their German co-workers.

At least there is no record that Fehler knew any of these facts. For he never mentions any of these items in his own war journal published by Werner Laurie of London in 1956 under the title *Dynamite for Hire*, with co-author A. V. Sellwood.

What Fehler did know, when his submarine left Kiel in the spring of 1945, was that the war in Europe would soon be over, and that Germany would lose. While the allies were deciding how to punish German war criminals, soldiers, sailors, and Nazi submarine captains, Fehler planned to be living a life of ease and luxury in a remote corner of the South Pacific, hunting wild pigs and sport fishing while sipping the finest German *Schnapps*. For in addition to a history-changing payload of nuclear weaponry, Fehler's surprising cargo included a three-year supply of food and fuel, sport rifles and shotguns, fishing tackle, and nearly 900 bottles of whiskey.

In his journal, Fehler reveals his ill-starred plan. He tried to recruit only single men for his crew, hoping they would not be as eager as married men to return to the Motherland. He said this part of his plan was sabotaged by the men themselves, for whenever the U-234 entered a port to make repairs or take on supplies or passengers, some of them would find themselves in relationships with local women whom they would promptly marry.

After all, the world was at war. Death waited at every corner. Young couples, raised in strict Christian circumstances, would marry in a heartbeat, knowing the most they might hope for was two or three days of wedded bliss. By the time the U-234 entered the deep waters of the Atlantic on its final voyage, nearly half the crew found themselves leaving wives and families behind.

Shortly after the war in Europe ended, while the U-234 was cruising through the warming waters of the South Atlantic, Captain Fehler told his officers, crew, and passengers that he was abandoning the mission to Japan. One of the passengers, a Nazi judge, and some of the young officers still loyal to the Third Reich, and two Japanese officers, were strongly opposed to the decision. Fehler explained his plan to find a South Pacific paradise, far out of reach of those who would punish German war criminals.

General Kessler, the highest ranking officer on board, was the only one who argued for surrender to the Americans. Based on interrogation reports made by U.S. military personnel after the surrender, it is apparent Kessler knew more about the nuclear weapons materials on board than did Fehler. Also, Kessler's loyalty to the Third Reich was suspect. Fehler believed Kessler was being sent to Japan as a form of exile. On the day the war ended the Nazi judge and one of the young officers were demanding Kessler be court-martialed for telling jokes at the expense of Nazi leaders, and refusing to celebrate Hitler's birthday.

In the end, Kessler pulled rank and got his way. Fehler abandoned his dream of an island vacation, turned the sub around, and headed for American waters. The Japanese officers committed suicide, and the Nazi judge finally shut his mouth.

Considering the above, it appears Johann Heinrich Fehler and Ulrich Kessler should have received a hero's welcome when they stepped onto American soil.

But the war in the Pacific was still raging. The American authorities classified all information concerning Fehler, his ship, cargo, mission, and passengers as top-secret "DUE TO VITAL IMPORTANCE TO PACIFIC WAR" as stated in a secret Naval communication.

For the most part, this information remained under wraps until the Freedom of Information Act was passed in 1990. The purpose of this book is to tell the story of Captain Fehler's epic voyage that could easily have changed the course of modern history had the U-234 completed its mission to Japan. And to serve as a gentle reminder that, as we are not ever completely sure of the capability of those who are trying to destroy us, we must be watchful and prepared.

Fehler himself probably didn't know what he had done as he walked down that lonely passageway toward the busses that would carry him to a prison cell. The rest of the world did not know either, and therefore could not understand or appreciate the significance of the U-234's surrender.

Chapter 2

In order to appreciate the significance of Fehler's cargo and his decision to turn it over to the Americans, a brief review of Germany's role in developing nuclear weapons is in order.

Following World War I, Germany lost its colonies and the natural resources which came from those colonies—not only coal and oil, but also rubber and minerals. German scientists were given the mandate to explore alternative sources of energy. *Ersatz* (substitute) energy, they called it.

Much of the research was conducted at the Kaiser Wilhelm Institute for Physics in Dahlem, a suburb of Berlin. Albert Einstein was named director of the institute in 1914. Working with him were well-known scientists Edward Teller, Fritz Strassman, Lise Meitner, Otto Hahn, Max Plank and J. Robert Oppenheimer.

Einstein was a theoretical physicist. He explained Brownian motion and the photoelectric effect, contributed to the theory of atomic spectra, and formulated the theories of special and general relativity ($E=mc^2$).

The early thirties brought changes to the institute. Some

of the scientists had to leave Germany to escape the persecution of the Jews by the Nazis. Some, including Einstein and Oppenheimer, went to the United States. Lise Meitner, a co-worker of Otto Hahn, went to Denmark to work with Niels Bohr, a Danish physicist.

New scientists filling the vacancies included Werner Heisenberg, Kurt Diebner, Erich Dagge, Karl Friedrich Weizaecker, and Manfred von Ardenne.

In December, 1938, Otto Hahn, after years of research, succeeded in splitting the uranium atom. The by-product was a burst of energy. His apparatus for splitting the first atom is on display today at the Deutsche Museum in Munich.

With Europe gearing up for another war, the most obvious application for Hahn's discovery was to develop a *Wunderwaffe*, the atom bomb. Knowing approximately how much energy was released with the splitting of a single atom, it didn't take Hahn long to figure that the splitting of atoms in twenty five or thirty kilogram masses of enriched uranium would have a greater explosive force than an entire train load of TNT.

He communicated his discovery to Lise Meitner and Niels Bohr in Denmark, before a scheduled trip by Bohr to the United States. In January, 1939, Bohr discussed Hahn's findings with Albert Einstein. In the summer of 1939, with support from L. Szilard, E. Witner and Einstein, Alexander Sachs presented the issue to President Franklin D. Roosevelt. In February 1940, $6,000 was made available to start fission research in the United States, and in June of 1942 the War Department organized the Manhattan Project under the direction of General Leslie Groves with Robert Oppenheimer as lead scientist.

In the meantime, Hahn, in the true spirit of scientific inquiry, published his findings, making them open to scientific scrutiny worldwide. Scientists anywhere in the world, including Japan, could read about his discovery, and try to duplicate his results. By 1940 physicists worldwide understood the theory for creating an atom bomb.

The big problem for those wanting to develop atom bombs was finding and producing fissionable material in kilogram quantities. While there was plenty of uranium in nature—found primarily in uraninite, pitchblende, tyuyamunite, carbonite, coffinite and autunite 99.3 percent of natural uranium was of the stable U-238 variety which could not be used in bombs. The unstable, fissionable uranium, U-235, also called enriched uranium, comprised only .7 percent of the ore in its natural state, and nobody yet knew how to separate one from the other in sufficient quantities to make bombs.

Another problem was developing a fuse system capable of starting the atomic chain reaction at pre-determined elevations in bombs dropped from airplanes.

The Americans were so eager to beat the Germans in this race of death and destruction, that they didn't notice a third party in the race, Japan. Under the leadership of Sakae Shimizu, Kyoto physicists were quietly laying the cornerstones for a Japanese atomic bomb.

In 1944, while the war in Europe was still raging, Otto Hahn was awarded the Nobel Prize in physics for his work in splitting the atom. He received his award after the war, in 1946 in Stockholm, Sweden.

Finding few uranium deposits on German soil, Hitler's scientists began looking for other sources of fissionable material, and made an unlikely discovery in the tailings of old silver and lead mines in a mountain range between Germany and Czechoslovakia, called Erzgebirge, in Saxony. Here the scientists found a brownish-black mineral containing Uraninite and Uranium trioxide, called pitchblende.

Thousands of German miners went to work. A mechanical, not chemical, separation process was developed, and by 1942 Germany was producing enriched uranium (U-235) in kilogram quantities.

In 1993 we received a letter from Dr. Manfred von Ardenne, one of the German scientists who was captured by the Russians and sent to Russia to help develop the first Soviet atom bomb. He sent us a copy of a picture of what he called the *Graaff-Atomumwandelungs-Anlage*, or *Trehnrohr*, perfected by Klaus Clusius and Gerhard Dickel in 1938. Similar to the separation equipment used in the petroleum industry, this new device consisted of two metal tubes with different diameters, one placed inside the other. The inner tube was heated, and the outer tube cooled. The lighter U-235 was attracted to the hot inner wall while the heavier U-238 was attracted to the cold outer wall. Convex currents created by this movement sent the U-235 upward and the U-238 downward. This was a simple and inexpensive method to produce large quantities of the unstable U-235 needed for the bombs. By 1942 Germany was far ahead of the United States in producing the enriched uranium needed for atomic weapons.

Germany did not build a reactor for the production of plutonium. This process required heavy water or graphite as a moderator. American scientists who concluded Germany could not produce atomic weapons without a heavy water production facility were only partly correct. Without heavy water the Germans could not produce large quantities of plutonium, but with their Trenrohr they could produce plenty of U-235 for Uranium bombs.

In the meantime, other German scientists were developing an infrared proximity fuse which included an altimeter so the new *Wunderwaffen* could be exploded at pre-set elevations.

The atomic research facility in Berlin-Dahlem was known to allied forces, and became the target of some of the bombing raids over Berlin. A safer place was built, an underground facility in the hills outside Stuttgart, near the towns of Haigerloch and Hechingen. Some of the elite scientists and physicists were assigned to this location, including Otto Hahn, Werner Heisenberg, Carl Friedrich von Weizacker, Max von Laue, Walter Gerlach, Max Plank, and Erich Dagge.

In addition, a third atomic research facility was established in Lichterfelde, near Berlin, under the direction of Dr. Manfred von Ardenne, with atomic scientists including Fritz Houterman, W. Bothe, H. Geiger, P. Harteck, Max Steenbeck, Peter Adolf Thiessen, Gernot Zippe, G. Hertz, Klaus Clusius and Gerhard Dickel. This facility quickly filled with sophisticated equipment, and the allies didn't know it was there.

At the end of the war in Europe, the Russians rounded up a hundred German scientists in the Berlin area and deported them to Moscow to build rockets and nuclear bombs. Without any help from the Americans, the Russians had their own atom bomb in just over three years after the war in Europe had ended.

With his eye on German scientists and technology, Stalin urged Eisenhower to stay at the Elbe River and let the Russian Army capture Berlin. This allowed the Russians to capture the Atom Research Center at Lichterfelde with all the sophisticated equipment, the pitchblende mines in what later became East Germany, and the German scientists working in and around Berlin, including von Ardenne, Steenbeck, Thiessen and Zippe who were instrumental in developing the atom bomb for the Soviet Union.

At the same time the Russians captured Kurt Magnus and his group of rocket scientists who had developed the A-4 rocket for the Soviets. After ten years most of these scientists were allowed to return to their homes in East Germany.

In 1993 we found Manfred von Ardenne at the Angewandte Medizinische Forshung, a cancer research center in Dresden, Saxony. In the correspondence that followed, he sent us thirty some odd pages of equations by Fritz Houterman, written in 1941, before the Manhattan Project was launched, containing exact formulas describing the chain reaction in atomic fission, and information about the new man-made element, plutonium (PU-239) which was also a fissionable material, used by the Americans in the second atom bomb dropped on Japan. (See Gary Sandquist letter at end of chapter 6.)

The question arises, that if the Germans knew so much about atom bombs, had an infrared proximity fuse, and were processing enriched uranium in kilogram quantities in the early 1940s, why didn't Adolf Hitler have the bomb first?

According to Manfred von Ardenne, the German scientists had become so soured on Adolf by the early forties, that they quietly decided among themselves that Hitler would not get the bomb. The discontent started with the persecution of the Jews in the early thirties, when scientists like Albert Einstein and Lise Meitner were forced to leave their homeland. Other Jewish scientists were sent to prison camps, never to be heard from again. A continuing harassment of the former German aristocracy also made waves in scientific circles.

The scientists knew that to oppose Hitler openly meant punishment and possibly death, so they quietly stalled. As the military pressed to receive the new bomb, there were always more tests to conduct and more technical problems still to be solved.

In the meantime, the two-billion-dollar Manhattan Project, under the direction of theoretical scientist J. Robert Oppenheimer and Major General Leslie Groves, was plunging forward.

The scope of the project leaped far beyond the wildest fantasies of the secret army of scientists and technicians who started it. Foreign-born physicists were everywhere.

The goal was to create a technological miracle to end the war. Teams of scientists worked around the clock at Columbia University in New York, the University of Chicago, and the University of California at Berkeley. Between March and June of 1942, the research army expanded from 45 to 1250 people. Eventually the project employed 125,000 people in the United States. Work moved forward with urgency, Oppenheimer and Groves believing the Germans were in the advanced stages of nuclear bomb development.

In 1942 Ernest Lawrence at the University of California came up with a separation process for uranium. He called his atom-smashing device the Calutron. When asked by a reporter how much U-235 he had separated, Lawrence proudly replied that in one month his laboratory had produced three samples of seventy five micrograms each, an infinitely small amount, and unstable U-235 comprised only 30 percent of the samples.

Upon enlarging his contraption to a mass spectrograph,

atom smashing jumped from morsels to larger morsels. The spectrograph separated a tenth of an ounce of U-235 a day. At this rate, the accumulation of the fifty kilograms necessary for a bomb would take fifty two years. Scientists in Hanford, Washington, were having better success producing plutonium.

In late 1943 and early 1944, the trickle of uranium and plutonium into the testing site of Los Alamos started growing. Gradually the trickle became a flow, and scientists began molding metal into warhead components–mostly plutonium because quantities were larger than that of uranium.

For the trigger, Oppenheimer originally planned a gun-type detonator—a pistol-looking device made of steel alloy, weighing about half a ton, six feet long, and with a threaded muzzle. The idea was to discharge a tiny bullet traveling at a speed of two thousand feet per second into a large "apple" of the fission core. The apple-bullet combination would create a super critical mass that would instantly chain react and explode, or so they hoped. They didn't have enough enriched uranium yet for testing, nor did they know how to adapt their pistol fuse for use on a moving airplane.

Once the fabrication and assembly of detonators and bomb parts were underway, Oppenheimer breathed a little more easily, thinking the Americans were finally ahead of the Germans. Michigan physicist Samuel Goudsmit reported the Germans were at least two years behind the Americans. He predicted that Hitler would be defeated using conventional weapons, and that Japan was not a threat. He didn't know the Germans had developed the infrared proximity fuse, that Germany already had hundreds of kilograms of enriched uranium ready for use, and that the Germans were actively using submarines to share information and materials with the Japanese.

The Americans were finally ready for a test in July, 1945. The assembled bomb device, called the Trinity, was hoisted to the top of a hundred-foot steel tower on Saturday, July 14, in the New Mexico desert.

After postponing the detonation because of thunderstorms, the first test firing was finally ready for countdown. At the base of the tower, scientist Morrison inserted the softball-sized plutonium core. The countdown began.

Zero hour was 5:29 a.m., Mountain War Time. For an instant, all was still. Fifteen seconds ahead of schedule, the thirty two lenses surrounding a grapefruit-sized plutonium core, brought it to a critical mass, allowing a runaway chain reaction of splitting atoms. In a few thousandths of a second, enough energy was released to recreate conditions similar to those in the explosion that gave birth to the universe. The fireball expanded. The mushroom cloud rose more than thirty thousand feet in a matter of seconds.

That same day, the heavy cruiser USS Indianapolis left Hunter's Point Naval Yard in San Francisco with two or more nuclear bombs, including the necessary uranium and fuses, and headed for the U.S. airbase on the Island of Tinian near Hawaii. The Americans were getting ready to show their new discovery to the Japanese.

In Japan, scientists had the same problems the Americans had, finding enough uranium to fuel their bombs. Prospecting expeditions were in vain until a General Tada found the precious commodity near Pau T'ou, in the Mukden-Dairen area of Manchuria. Later, excavations took place in the Anshan area south of Mukden. There Tada discovered a crystalline rock with Uranium ore called pegmatite.

Using this ore, physicist Suzuki, with fifty experts from the army and top universities, extracted eleven pounds of enriched uranium, far short of what was needed to produce an effective bomb. They blamed their failures on poor equipment, lack of money and a shortage of materials. Laboratory methods for splitting the uranium atoms were behind the times. Japan was forced to rely more and more on German technology.

For example, Japan had built an ultra-centrifuge for separating isotopes. This machine ran at 100,000 to 150,000 rpms for minimal operation. At these high speeds, however, breakdowns were frequent, and uranium gas was produced, which ate through almost any metal. German scientists provided a special steel shield which seemed impervious to the gas.

In declassified German records from the Kriegs Tage Buch (daily war journal, KTB) from German naval headquarters for the Atlantic, headed by Admiral Karl Doenitz, U-boats operating under the code name Tanne would rendezvous with Japanese submarines in the south Atlantic where equipment, technology and people were transferred to the Japanese subs on a fairly frequent basis.

KTB entries dated June 9 and June 26, 1944, explicitly discuss transferring special equipment and several German scientists to Japanese vessels. Kapitanleutnant Kurt Lange of the German submarine U-530 navigated such missions. Also, in April 1945, the U-843, under Commander Oskar Herwartz, returned from a trip to Japan.

As teacher to student, Germany shared its secrets and

technology with Japan, hoping to strengthen Japan's chances for global domination.

Japan had the foresight to know Germany had something very big, and did everything it could to become a dominant player in the nuclear bomb race.

Chapter 3

The growing unrest among the elite in Hitler's Third Reich came to a climax on July 20, 1944. A small high-wing monoplane, named the Fieseler Storch, left Berlin. Its destination was the Wolf's Lair, Hitler's secret getaway, a place hidden in a forest near the city of Rastenburg, East Prussia.

A staff meeting was scheduled at noon, with Adolf Hitler in charge. Oberst Graf Schenk von Stauffenberg, a staff member scheduled to attend the meeting, was on the plane, as well as the pilot, Feldwebel Neumann and two ordinance officers. Stauffenberg was paying more attention to his briefcase this morning than was usual. It contained a time bomb installed by ordinance experts in Berlin.

Stauffenberg was outwardly calm, but many thoughts were passing through his mind. If everything went according to plan, Hitler would be dead in less than an hour. The pilot and ordinance officers also knew about the bomb.

Back in Berlin, a co-conspirator, Major Remer, was preparing his troops to take possession of the government headquarters at Wilhelmstrasse as soon as news arrived that Hitler was dead.

The plane arrived at the Wolf's Lair just prior to the 12:30 meeting. There was little time to mingle with other staff members.

While Stauffenberg headed for the conference room, the pilot and ordinance officers remained at the plane, ready for a quick departure back to Berlin.

A huge oak conference table with thick, solid legs, occupied the center of the room. Maps covered the table. Staff members were standing about, chatting with one another.

Stauffenberg placed the briefcase under the table close to the spot where Hitler was known to stand in earlier meetings. The briefcase was leaning against a solid table support as Stauffenberg activated the timer switch.

When Hitler and additional staff members entered the room, Stauffenberg excused himself, and headed for the waiting airplane.

As Hitler began the meeting, he became annoyed when he accidentally kicked the briefcase under the table. One of the officers quickly moved the briefcase to the other side of the oak support where it would be out of the way.

As the meeting moved into high gear, maps were moved about the table as the staff studied the Russian and German positions along the eastern front. So far, not a single Russian soldier had crossed the German border. Hitler was trying to convince his generals that Germany still had a good chance to win the war on the eastern front.

At 12:42 the bomb exploded. The room was in shambles. Several staff members were dead, the rest wounded. But Hitler, the intended target, was only slightly hurt. The heavy oak support had absorbed most of the blast and shrapnel. Hitler was in shock, but otherwise healthy.

In the meantime small groups of soldiers were showing up at the Reichskanzlei at Wilhelmstrasse to take possession of the building. But Josef Goebbels, who was in the office, had already been informed in a message from the Wolf's Lair that the attempt on Hitler's life had failed. Goebbels had orders to spare no mercy in eliminating the participants, or suspected participants, in the plot.

SS and Gestapo troopers were soon in control, mercilessly killing all German soldiers who tried to approach the building.

Upon arrival in Berlin, Oberst Stauffenberg, the man who had planted the bomb at the Wolf's Lair, was taken into custody and held at the Kommando Dienstelle at Bendlerstrasse. Stauffenberg, General Olbricht and other high ranking German officers were taken out behind the building and shot that same afternoon.

General Oberst Fromm was arrested by Heinrich Himmler and shot on August 7. General Oberst Ludwig Beck, who was supposed to take over the government in the event the assassination was a success, took his own life.

On August 7 and 8, 1944, Judge Ronald Freisler pronounced the death sentence on the following German officers: Field Marshall von Witzleben, General Hoepner, General Stief, General von Hase, junior officers Hagen, Klausing, Bernardis and Count Peter York von Wartenburg. These men were executed on August 8 at the Ploetzensee Prison in Berlin.

Hitler ordered that the guilty parties be hanged like cattle, the sentences to be carried out by strangulation using piano wire strung from meat hooks. The eight men were herded into a small room in which eight meat hooks hung from the ceiling. One by one, after being stripped to the waist, they were strung up. Tourists visiting the Ploetzensee Prison today can look in the small room where the meat hooks are still hanging.

But Hitler wasn't satisfied. After the attempt on his life he didn't trust anyone. From August, 1944 until April, 1945, 4,980 German soldiers, officers, generals and civilians were executed by Himmler's Gestapo and SS troops for possible involvement in the attempted bombing at the Wolf's Lair.

Tens of thousands of German soldiers were being slaughtered on the Russian front as German positions collapsed. German soldiers in France were being uprooted, slaughtered, or captured by advancing allied forces. Thousands of German civilians were dying as American and British bombs were dropping on German cities and towns, almost nightly. Now Hitler was adding to the death toll by killing nearly five thousand key military and civilian personnel himself, because he thought they might have been involved in the bomb plot at the Wolf's Lair.

Two conclusions can be made from Hitler's ruthless purge. Hitler had an unbridled passion for revenge. If he was willing to murder five thousand of his top men for possible involvement in an attempt on his life, what kind of passion would he have to seek revenge on the Russians and Americans who were destroying his precious Third Reich? His Army was no longer an effective tool for seeking revenge on his enemies, but what about his nuclear scientists who were very close to producing atom bombs? If the bomb became available too late to be used by the German army, who else would be willing to use it to punish the Americans? The Japanese, of course.

Also, with the attempt on Hitler's life by insiders, and the following purge or murder of five thousand of his top people,

Hitler finally had to face the reality that his government and war machine were disintegrating. With Russian armies advancing from the east, and the Americans coming from the west, it was only a matter of time, perhaps less than a year, when the war in Europe would end with Germany's surrender.

Leaders of the Third Reich, and certainly Adolf Hitler, would not be treated kindly by the victors, especially after news of the Jewish genocide was made public. It was time to make escape plans. Hitler was not a man to put a gun to his head or go down with the ship—not if safer, more prudent options were available.

Chapter 4

During the war years, Nazi leadership had accumulated large amounts of loot or booty from the countries they had captured. The booty included gold, silver, jewelry, and precious stones.

Seeing his Third Reich begin to crumble, it seems only logical that Hitler would start looking for ways out of the country, and a method to get his booty out too. It is unlikely he would just leave his treasure behind for the Russians or Americans to capture.

Martin Bormann, Reichleiter and secretary to Adolf Hitler, always seemed to be lingering in the shadow of his master. Plus he seemed to be out of favor with his jealous associates: Himmler, Speer, Goering, and Goebbels. Hitler trusted Bormann, who more than anyone else was familiar with the captured treasures.

Hitler selected Bormann to oversee the shipment of booty to a safer place, not a simple task considering the onslaught of the allies on all sides, and the fact that many of the former German-friendly countries had declared war on Germany when they realized the tide was turning against the

Third Reich. Brazil declared war on Germany in August 1942, and Argentina as late as March, 1945.

But this didn't deter Bormann who had already established good connections in Argentina through a Spanish agent named Alcazar de Valasco. The Spaniard apparently had close ties with Juan Peron and Evita Duarte, who later became Peron's wife and first lady.

General Wilhelm Faupel, a former ambassador to Argentina, now stationed in Madrid, arranged for docking and storage facilities for German submarines in the Spanish city of Cadiz.

As early as 1943, de Valasco assured Bormann that Argentina would not only provide a hiding place for booty, but for Nazis as well. The secret operation overseeing the shipments of treasure and people to Argentina was given the code name Feuerland.

Two U-boats were assigned to Operation Feuerland, the U-530 and the U-977. Commander of the U-530, Kurt Lange, later replaced by Otto Wermuth, was given the fastest U-boat in the German navy. S. Heinz Schaefer commanded the U-977.

To help with the Feuerland mission, Bormann selected three men who had connections with Germans living in Argentina: General Wilhelm Faupel, a former Argentine ambassador now stationed in Madrid; Gottfried Sandstede who had been forced to flee Buenos Aires earlier; and Captain Dietrich Niebuhr, expelled from Argentina in 1941 for espionage.

Sandstede and Faupel joined up with Niebuhr, who was already stationed in Spain, and together the three boarded a U-boat for Argentina.

Ludwig Freude, a lieutenant in the Argentine naval

reserve made it possible for Bormann's team to enter Buenos Aires where they met Dr. Heinrich Doerge, a consultant with the Central Bank of Argentina; Richard von Leute, general manager of the huge Lahousen Ranch; and Evita Duarte.

Freude and his German visitors selected four banks to handle the treasures of the Third Reich: Banco Aleman-Transatlantic, The Banco Tornquist, The Banco Alemano, and The Banco Germanico.

One can only guess at the size of the treasure accumulated by German troops as they occupied France, Belgium, Denmark, Austria, The Netherlands, Poland, etc. It was certainly in the millions, possibly valued at billions of dollars. It was large enough that the facilities of at least four banks were needed to stash it away.

Evita Duarte was a young actress of questionable reputation when Freude asked her to be part of his group. Later, when she became Argentina's first lady, she was called The Little Madonna. While helping the Germans, she already had a relationship with Colonel Juan Domingo Peron, her future husband. Evita eventually handled transactions for Operation Feuerland, lending her name to those transactions.

Bormann was pleased when Faupel and Sandstede reported their progress. One can only guess who besides Hitler and Bormann might be beneficiaries of the vast German treasure. Certainly Freude and Evita Duarte received generous commissions.

The transfer of treasure from Berlin to Argentina cannot be looked upon as the fumbling of a lunatic, but a well-conceived and executed plan to help ensure the prosperity and safety of high-ranking Nazis able to flee the final collapse of the Third Reich.

Chapter 5

It was Martin Bormann and Admiral Karl Doenitz, who commanded the German Navy in the Atlantic, who planned what was called the Northern Escape Route.

Beginning in 1944 selected U-boats at Kiel and other German ports were refitted with larger fuel and freight capacities and passenger compartments.

These modifications were completed in late 1944, and 1945.

In a U.S. interrogation report, dated May 24, 1945, General Ulrich Kessler, who had arrived in Portsmouth with Johann Fehler on the U-234, said that the mission of the U-234 was to help Japan win the war in the Pacific.

The plan was launched in December, 1944, in Berlin-Dahlem. In addition to German officials, Japanese representatives included ambassador to Germany, Hideo Tomonaga, Oshima Hiroshi, and Fregatten kaptain Genzo Shoji. At this meeting the Germans offered Japan the Third Reich's most advanced weaponry, some of it still in the development stage, such as the atomic bomb with accompanying infrared proximity fuses and enough enriched uranium for a dozen explosions.

Also offered were the plans and weapons which enabled the German air defense system to shoot down over eight thousand American bombers. Germany expressed a willingness to ship the weapons and plans to Japan on U-boats along with German scientists and personnel to help develop and implement the use of the new weapons.

There is no record of what the Japanese might have paid for this package which could possibly lead to world conquest. Cash-poor Japan might have paid for it handsomely, well aware that it was just a matter of time until the Americans would also have atomic weapons. Least of all, the Japanese would have promised Hitler and his associates a piece of the post-war world if the new weapons were useful in defeating the Americans.

According to a memorandum from the office of the chief of naval operations in Washington D.C., Nazi judge Kay Nieschling, a passenger on the U-234, revealed the following in a July 27, 1945 interrogation. He said Fregattenkapitan Gerhard Falck was the chief technician, under Admiral Wennecker, in charge of all naval matters concerning the secret shipment to Japan. Falck was involved in a number of secret training sessions before boarding the U-234.

Nieschling said a Nazi named Bicker was responsible for contacting the various German agencies regarding what and how much was to be included in the cargo. He added the names of other German and Japanese officials involved in cargo selection.

The only person in the entire Third Reich with enough power to authorize such a mission was Adolph Hitler himself.

As the war in Europe was drawing to a close it is probable that any hard cash or gold the Japanese might have paid would have been routed to the bank vaults in Argentina instead of Berlin.

Japan was losing the war in the Pacific, and needed a miracle. Hitler had missed the chance to use the new *Wunderwaffe* in Europe, but with a little luck the Japanese would be able to use it in the Pacific. With the American ships assembling for the invasion of Japan, a wonderful opportunity for the first use of nuclear weapons was presenting itself. A couple of nukes exploded at high elevation would sink hundreds, if not thousands of American ships. Another bomb or two dropped on Los Angeles and San Francisco, and the Americans would be begging for peace, with Japan dictating the terms.

Chapter 6

The voyage of the U-234 with its unusual cargo is one of the last great secrets of the Third Reich, a secret that the allies continued to keep under wraps even after the war ended.

To deliver this precious cargo to the Japanese, Admiral Doenitz selected a brand new XB mine-laying sub that had never seen active service. The U-234 and her twin, the U233, were the largest U-boats in the German navy, approximately ninety meters long. The surface speed was twenty knots. Underwater they could travel at twelve knots, and could submerge to a depth of three hundred meters.

Johann Heinrich Fehler, the decorated officer from the raider Atlantis was made skipper. The U-234 had five officers and fifty-one crew members. Crew and officers had to report to duty in Kiel early in 1944, a full year before the targeted departure date. Fehler took his new ship and crew on practice maneuvers in the Baltic Sea to get acquainted with this large vessel and its recent modifications. None of them knew about the secret mission to Japan.

General Ulrich Kessler, former chief of staff of the Luftwaffe, learned of the mission at Berchtesgaden in 1944, where he was told the Fuehrer planned to help Japan win the war in the Pacific by giving them a special weapon.

The cargo manifest included 13.5 kilograms of bomb fuses and 560 kilograms of uranium oxide (U-235), an enriched uranium ready to be used in bombs.

Carrying highly radioactive uranium from Germany to Japan created a problem. The crew had to be shielded from the radiation. The uranium was divided into ten equal parts of 56 kilograms each to be enclosed in steel cylinders lined with solid gold. (See Dr. Gary Sandquist letter at end of chapter.)

The ten cylinders were designed to fit into the vertical mine-laying shafts located on both sides of the boat. If any of the cylinders developed radiation leaks, the faulty container could be released and allowed to fall to the bottom of the ocean.

According to the log book, the U-234 glided into the submarine bunker at Kiel in early March, 1944, and started loading its Japan-bound cargo. Second officer, Karl Pfaff, was in charge of loading the cargo. Besides the sophisticated weaponry there were large crates carrying two disassembled turbojet fighters, the Messerschmidt 262 and 163.

There was one cargo item, however, that had a questionable value in helping Japan win the war. Pfaff supervised the loading of nine hundred bottles of Schnapps or whiskey, much more than Fehler and his staff could reasonably consume during the voyage.

According to a handwritten note from second mate Pfaff, the U-234 wasn't the only German U-boat waiting to take passengers and freight to foreign shores. He lists the following:

U-2511–Commander Schness, boat type XXI, the most modern German U-boat.

U-874–Commander Preuss, boat type IX D, waiting for her guests.

U-875–Commander Petersen, Boat type IX D2, waiting for her guests.

U-8___–Commander Bahn, boat type IX D2, waiting for her guests.

Pfaff didn't mention the U-530 and U-977 which were also retooled to haul passengers. Perhaps these two U-boats had already departed, were waiting for their passengers at another port, or had entirely different missions.

Otto Wermuth, commander of the U-530 later said that his boat was in Christiansand, Norway during the later part of April, 1945. Heinze Schaeffer, commander of the U-977, made a similar statement.

Compared to the other U-boats, the U-234 had three times the cargo capacity, plus it had the modifications for carrying extra passengers. All we have is a brief statement from one of the crewmen that twelve unidentified passengers met the boat at Christiansand. Plus we have a log entry describing the circumstances surrounding the exit of the unnamed passengers off the coast of Argentina prior to surrender. We could find no further clues as to who these passengers might have been, and we could find no evidence that any of the crew or officers revealed the identity of any of these passengers to the Americans after their surrender.

In 1960, Alcazar de Velasco, the Nazi agent in Spain, who coordinated the shipments of Nazi booty to Argentina, published a book in which he claimed he personally escorted

Martin Bormann to Argentina in a German submarine.

Many wanted Nazis disappeared from Germany during this same time period, but the officers and crewmen of the passenger U-boats never revealed the identity of their passengers. Maybe they didn't know. Perhaps the names of the passengers were withheld, even from the officers and crew.

Retooled U-boats were ordered by Admiral Doenitz to remain offshore and available for weeks, even months, in the event top Nazis had to use them to escape FBI agents and Allied troops. According to the Kriegs Tage Buch (KTB) the U-530 surrendered at Mar del Plata, Argentina on July 10, 1945, two months after the war in Europe had ended, and one month before the atom bombs dropped on Japan. The U-977 surrendered at the same Argentine port, August 17, 1945.

Officers and crewmen of both boats were interrogated by Argentine authorities to determine what they were doing in Argentine waters, but without success. After several weeks Captain Wermuth and his crew were sent to a U.S. prison camp for further interrogation. Answers were carefully rehearsed, and the truth did not come forth.

Skipper Wermuth was kept in solitary confinement during his interrogation. After more than six months he was sent to England to face British interrogators, who were no more successful than the American and Argentine authorities.

Captain Schaeffer of the U-977, eventually ended up in England too, but he didn't talk either. Years later Schaeffer gave the following explanation:

"We all, officers and crewmen, had kept our secrecy, not that we did any wrong, we followed orders, and we, never Nazis, fought unpolitically for our beloved Germany, for her very survival. What will be accomplished by telling what the real mission was? Let this matter sleep, along with our faithful U-boats at the bottom of the Atlantic..."

The U-234 had special orders to continue its voyage to Japan after dropping off its passengers in Argentina, even if the war in Europe was over.

16 April 2001

To Whom It May Concern:

I am Gary M. Sandquist, Professor and director of Nuclear Engineering at the University of Utah in Salt Lake City, Utah. I have been asked by A.O. Naujoks and Lee Nelson, Authors of the book "The Last Great Secret of the Third Reich," to provide an assessment and this statement regarding certain materials which were reportedly aboard the German Submarine designated as "U-234" which surrendered to the US in 1945. This German Submarine and its cargo and purpose is the major focus of their book.

This German Submarine was apparently assigned a special mission to transport certain personnel and materials from Germany to Japan in spring of 1945. According to the manifest found on the U-234, this boat carried 560 kilograms (1,120 pounds) of Uranium (referenced as uranium oxide) produced in Germany and being transported to Japan. Also a shipping crate with bomb fuses (purportedly proximity fuses) was part of the cargo. The boat also had on board a group of (seven) highly trained Scientists, headed by a German Major General.

It is difficult without more complete information to fully assess the purpose of these materials and intent of the Germans and Japanese in making this unusual exchange at the close of the Second World War in Europe. The Authors have obtained certain records now declassified from the Library of Congress. Complete documentation regarding the actual events and circumstances are not available. The records that the Authors have obtained indicate that the materials reported in the manifest included 560 kilograms of uranium oxide that was packed into at least ten separate "gold-lined" cylinders and carefully sealed. A statement by a crewmember of the subma-

41

rine indicated that the cylinders should not be opened because of "potential dangerous reactions."

The following statements provide speculation by me regarding the nature and possible purpose of these materials and personnel aboard U-234 dispatched to Japan. A secret message from United States Chief of Naval Operations (CNO) to the New York Port Authority (NYPORT) dated 27 May 1945 stating that the material was "uranium oxide" is perplexing. Uranium oxide (UO2 or U3O8) are the stable forms of uranium found in nature. Chemically both of these compounds of uranium are stable and unreactive. However, any isotope of uranium metal is highly "pyrophoric." Any isotope of pure uranium metal can spontaneously ignite and burn in the presence of oxygen. The US employed such depleted uranium metal for munitions used against Iraqi tanks during the "Desert Storm" campaign.

There are also statements implying that the uranium was enriched which implies that the content of the isotope U-235 was increased in the material at a level greater than its natural occurrence of about 0.7%. It is well known that uranium metal enriched to about 90% in U-235 is considered suitable for producing atomic weapons. Whether the Germans had actually been able to enrich uranium to such a degree is unknown. There is documented evidence that German scientists had developed a process for isotope enrichment called "thermal diffusion" as early as 1941.

The official US position has been that Germany was unsuccessful in any of its major efforts in producing an atom bomb. This included the assumption that the Germans did not produce either plutonium-239 which is made in special nuclear reactors or enriched uranium in U-235 which requires some means for separating isotopes of natural uranium. Enrichment of uranium or production of Pu-239 is required to achieve a nuclear weapon.

However, the fact that the German Submarine transported its uranium cargo in at least ten separate containers and these containers were sealed and gold-lined would seem to indicate that the uranium was in a metallic (very reactive) form. Furthermore the material may have been enriched in U-

235. It is logical that the several canisters with such unusual configurations (long thin rods) rather than one large canister were used to preclude criticality of the enriched uranium material during shipment to Japan. To prevent accidental criticality of fissile materials (U-235 or Pu-239) such fissile materials are configured in geometries to enhance neutron leakage and parasitic absorption. Interestingly, gold is a strong neutron absorber and may have been placed in the canisters to absorb neutrons.

If this uranium material was indeed enriched in U-235 the Japanese with the assistance of German scientists could have quickly fabricated atomic bombs of the so-called "gun shot" design. An inventory of 560 kilograms of enriched U-235 (at 90% or greater enrichment) could have provided the Japanese with an arsenal of a dozen or more "Hiroshima class atom bombs."

The assumption that the Germans made little or no progress in their attempts to build an atom bomb should be carefully reassessed. Otto Hahn and Fritz Strassmann were German Chemists who first achieved nuclear fission in 1938. It was their discovery and information leaked to the world that began the efforts by the English, French and the U.S. to build such formidable weapons. It has been assumed that only the U.S. had the major resources and safety from external threats of bombing and sabotage to successfully complete such a demanding effort. The U.S. expended over 2 billion dollars on its program to build the bomb called the "Manhattan Project."

However, it is important to remember that even with constant bombing of German industries and infrastructure, the Germans were able to develop rockets, jet aircraft, superior tanks, synthetic fuels, and other military materials while still waging a major conflict on two fronts.

Sincerely

Professor Gary M. Sandquist, Ph.D., PE
Director of Nuclear Engineering
University of Utah
Salt Lake City, Utah, USA

43

Chapter 7

The question arises as to how escaping Nazis, including Hitler and Bormann, could reach the waiting submarines, when Berlin was surrounded by the Russian Army. They flew.

Hanna Reitsch was born in Hirschberg, Silesia in 1912. She is an unsung hero in aviation history. Prior to the outbreak of World War II, she was a test pilot, flying mostly gliders, not only in Germany, but other countries as well.

By the time the war started, Hanna had a brilliant reputation among Luftwaffe officers. Word of her talented flying reached General Ernst Udet who officially recruited her. Eventually she became a test pilot for revamped V-1 rockets.

Hanna responded to frequent urgent requests to fly, sometimes in the middle of allied air attacks. Never refusing her orders, she became obsessed with the guardianship of Hitler and his top officials. She was decorated with the E.K. I (First Class Iron Cross) and the E.K. II (Second Class Iron Cross), which were presented to her personally by Adolf Hitler and Hermann Goering. There is some speculation that she was romantically involved with Hitler.

Hanna wasn't far from Hitler during the final days of the

war. In her diaries, published in two books, *Fliegen, Mein Leben,* and *Das Unzerstoerbare in Meinem Leben* (both in German language only) she recalls flying in and out of Berlin during the last months of the war. Hanna was wounded trying to get to a shelter during an allied bombing raid over Berlin in October 1944. While in the hospital she met Luftwaffe flying ace, Oberst Hans Ulrich Rudel, who had just lost a leg by amputation.

Recognizing the deteriorating condition of the war, they decided it would be a good idea to begin making plans for low-level flights, without radar, in and out of Berlin.

Upon release from the hospital Hanna began memorizing recognizable landmarks in and around Berlin which would enable her to make low-level flights including landings and takeoffs in marginal light and weather conditions. Rudel made Luftwaffe officials aware of her efforts.

That winter Hanna was released from duty to return to her family in Kitzbuehl, Austria. She thought her efforts to prepare for emergency flights in and out of Berlin had been in vain.

Then in April, 1945, she received a call from the commander of the Luftwaffe, Generaloberst von Greim, who was in Munich, asking her to fly him to Berlin where she was to receive a special assignment. A J-188 aircraft was waiting for them at the Munich airport.

At the deserted Gato airport near Berlin they changed planes, Hanna taking the controls of a Fiesler Storch. By this time the Russians had surrounded the German capital, making it necessary to fly over enemy territory on their way to the designated landing strip, located between the Brandenburg Gate and the Column of Victory, near Hitler's bunker.

It was late afternoon when they left Gato. Hanna had the flight pattern in her head. In the distance she could see the smoke and dust of Berlin. Some of the landmarks she had memorized were now gone, the result of allied bombs and Russian artillery. She flew at treetop level to avoid enemy radar and artillery.

While passing over the Grunewald, a wooded area west of Berlin, she could see hundreds of Russian soldiers grabbing their rifles so they could begin shooting at her. Anti-aircraft guns began firing too.

A piece of shrapnel hit General Greim in the leg. Another piece hit the fuel tank. The general passed out. His wound was bleeding badly. Hanna couldn't help because her hands were needed on the controls.

When she saw the Column of Victory, the firing of rifles and anti-aircraft guns had stopped. She was over friendly territory. The motor was beginning to sputter from lack of fuel. Finally she was down, taxiing toward the Brandenburg Gate.

Greim was taken to Hitler's bunker where his leg was operated on. While he was recovering, Hitler promoted him to General Feldmarschall and commander of the Luftwaffe to replace Goering who, with his staff, had already departed to an unknown destination.

Hanna describes one of the flights in her diary.

A personnel carrier takes me and Ritter von Greim back to the Brandenburg Gate. The plane is ready for takeoff. It was still dark over the city. At this time, most soldiers are napping in their foxholes. The sky was painted in red from large fires raging in the city of Berlin. After takeoff, several Russian anti-aircraft guns are giving us some static moments, but at 1700 meters, we are lucky. There is a cloud cover, and we are safe. Above these clouds, a clear sky with shimmering stars. I take course north by northwest to reach the airport at Rechlin. (Located at the south end of the Mueritz See.) At this base, camouflaged and hidden under trees, some of the Luftwaffe's latest airplanes were on standby, as well as a contingent of German fighter planes to fly escort.

General von Greim is under much pain and would like to fly back to Salzburg, but I have to overrule Ritter von Greim. I have a message for Gross-Admiral Doenitz (commander of the Atlantic navy) which I have to convey personally to him.

At that time Doenitz maintained his headquarters in Ploen, a few miles south of Kiel. Upon leaving Rechlin, Hanna flew at treetop level to Ploen.

Albert Speer, who visited Hitler during this same time period, described his last flight out of Berlin. He said planes arrived and departed at dawn and dusk, when visibility was poor. The pilots could barely see, and did not use running or landing lights.

The previously mentioned landing strip, used by Hanna Reitsch, was approximately five hundred yards from Hitler's bunker, near the Brandenburg Gate. The wide boulevard, called the Ost-West Achse, leading from the Brandenburg Gate to the Victory Column, was the runway used by Hanna Reitsch.

A maintenance crew stationed in basements of nearby buildings alongside the airstrip kept the air traffic going. Whenever an enemy shell would hit this strip, the hole was filled and graded as quickly as possible. The Brandenburg Gate itself served as a kind of hangar, supplied with barrels of aviation fuel, a filling station and a crew of mechanics. A camouflage canopy was stretched across the runway near the Brandenburg Gate so stationary aircraft could not be seen from the air by enemy bombers.

At dusk the maintenance crew would place red kerosene lanterns along the runway so aircraft could land in the dark. In the morning the lanterns were removed.

Once the airstrip was in operation, high-ranking officers and Nazi leaders came and went at will. The Fiesler Storch was a high-wing monoplane that had no trouble landing on less than perfect surfaces.

After the war, Hanna was locked up in solitary confinement for eighteen months. She repeatedly refused to discuss her flights in and out of Berlin during the final days of the war.

When the war was over, General Feldmarschall Ritter von Greim was taken into custody. He committed suicide in his prison cell in Salzburg.

Hanna Reitsch revealed the following at the end of her diary:

I received royal treatment from the U.S. Army. They invited me to live in a plush villa at Gmund, Austria. But this treatment lasted only a short time.

After the days of wine and roses, I was transferred to Freising and Oberursal in Germany, a prison camp. I was kept for eighteen months without trial, in solitary confinement. My interrogator (U.S. intelligence officer) was mostly interested in my flights in and out of Berlin. The main question he repeatedly asked: Was I involved in flying Nazis and the Hitlers out of Berlin? All I would tell him was my name, and a description of my duty as a German who loved her fatherland.

I think the statements made by Erich Kempka, Hitler's

Chauffeur, who told how he burned the Hitlers, were accepted. Why was I kept in solitary confinement and asked over and over again whether I was involved in flying the Hitlers out of Berlin? Before I was transferred to a prison cell, I had a chance to meet my family. The only thing I found was seven fresh graves, in Salzburg. Every member of my family had committed suicide. But I tried to stay alive, and I did. I was now a prisoner of the U.S. occupation forces. After my refusal to cooperate, the face of America turned ugly. What was my wrongdoing or crime? I was a German, a woman, a pilot who fulfilled her moral obligations.

Regarding the legend of my flights in and out of Berlin and the possibility of flying out the Hitlers, I have no comments...

Hitler's chauffeur, Erich Kempka, told interrogators that the Hitlers had committed suicide in their bunker, and that Kempka had dragged the bodies outside and cremated them in a bomb crater by pouring gasoline over them. This is the story sold by the Americans to the entire world.

Joseph Stalin, who had first access to the bunker because his troops captured Berlin, believed Hitler had escaped to South America or Japan.

The fact that Hanna Reitsch, Johann Fehler, and the other two U-boat captains faced continuing interrogation with questions concerning the whereabouts of Hitler for nearly two years following the close of the war certainly supports Stalin's belief that Hitler had escaped.

Consider the collapse of Berlin. In the spring of 1945 most of the city was in ruins from the incessant bombing.

Stalin and Eisenhower had already made a deal in which the Americans agreed to stop their advancing troops at the Elbe

River so the Russians could take Berlin all by themselves. How Stalin was able to convince Eisenhower that this was a sensible course of action we may never know. If the Americans had taken Berlin, the post war splitting of the city with the Berlin Wall and Checkpoint Charlie might never have happened.

With the Russian capture of Berlin, uranium processing facilities, and the atomic laboratory at Berlin Lichterfelde fell into Russian hands along with the uranium mines in what later became East Germany. The Russians now had everything they needed to build their own nuclear arsenal, without the help of Americans, including spies.

In April, 1945, Berlin was surrounded by Russian troops inching their way toward Wilhelmstrasse where Hitler's bunker was located; the same soldiers who had repeatedly fired at Hanna Reitsch as she flew in and out of Berlin.

General Weidling and SS-Brigadefuehrer Mohnke were in charge of the defense of the city. Most of the regular soldiers at this point in time were either captured or killed near the American and Russian fronts, and the only men left to maintain the last defense at Berlin were boys from the Hitler Jugend organization and old men from the Volks Sturm Units. Berlin's defenders had some tanks and artillery pieces, but these were mostly useless from lack of ammunition.

Downtown Berlin was situated between the Spree River and the Landwehr Canal. Russian troops were positioned on the northern bank of the Spree and on the southern bank of the Landwehr Canal. The Russians were moving slowly, not fearing the German troops as much as the many mines and bombs which they knew were waiting for them.

Reitsch mentions in her diary that during the last days Hitler discovered a way to delay the Russian advance at least another twenty-four hours. He decided to bomb the city's Landwehr Canal and nearby flood-prevention locks, at a point where the canal passed over one of the S-Bahn (subway) tunnels, thereby allowing the water to enter the tunnel and flood Berlin's downtown S-Bahn and U-Bahn system. Another charge was placed where six S-Bahn lines intersected at Trebbiner Strasse.

Those who planned the flooding of the subway tunnels undoubtedly knew that thousands of women, children and wounded German soldiers had entered the tunnels to seek refuge from the American bombs and Russian artillery, and to wait for the war to end. The women and children were huddled in dark, cold corners and along the stone walls, while most of the wounded soldiers were resting on railroad cars parked on abandoned underground tracks.

We do not know who gave the final order, only that it happened in the pre-dawn hours on an April day, 1945. After the explosions shook the city, millions of gallons of cold river water rushed into the tunnels, killing many thousands of Germans.

It is impossible to estimate the exact number of casualties. As the water continued to flow, many of the bodies were washed out of the tunnels and into the river to disappear forever.

Hearing the new explosions, the Russians slowed down their approach to the city, not sure what the Germans were up to. Russian casualties had been high while approaching the outskirts of Berlin, and they anticipated a terrible resistance inside the city.

The shooting stopped and the city capitulated on May 2, 1945. Civilians and soldiers entered the streets to meet their

Russian captors.

On May 2, at 8:23 a.m., General Hellmuth Weidling, defense commander of Berlin, signed a cease-fire with the Russians.

By 9 a.m. Russian troops entered Hitler's bunker. At the time many high ranking German officers and numerous German soldiers were being disarmed by the Russians. But Martin Bormann, many other Nazi leaders, and members of Hitler's staff could not be found.

While searching Hitler's bunker Russians found the bodies of several German generals and the entire family of Josef Goebbels. All had taken their own lives.

None of Hitler's personal staff ever faced a Russian soldier. Some were found after the war in the western part of Germany, including Mr. Manzialy, the vegetarian cook, secretaries Mrs. Christian and Miss Krueger, and chauffeur Erich Kempka.

The bunker was made of steel and concrete, and was safe against heavy bombardments. It had several levels. Hitler's living quarters were on the lower floor where allied reports later claimed Hitler shot himself in the head with his pistol. His wife Eva Braun swallowed poison.

The most accepted version of the suicide had Hitler sitting in the middle of the room, holding his Walther 7.65 pistol in his hand while Eva reclined on the sofa drinking her poison.

According to some theories, Hitler placed the pistol barrel in his mouth and pulled the trigger. Such a bullet would have passed through the brain and left a large hole exiting the top or back of the skull. Blood and particles of brain and bone would have splattered on the concrete walls. The bullet would have maintained sufficient velocity to make a mark where it struck the concrete.

The Russians found no blood, no particles of tissue, and no bullet mark on the walls or ceiling.

Hitler's chauffeur, Erich Kempka, later captured by the allies, claimed he dragged the bodies of Adolf and Eva outside on April 30, placed them in a bomb crater, poured gasoline over them, and cremated them.

Any crematorium technician will tell you that in order for cremation to take place the body needs to be placed in an enclosure where a temperature over three thousand degrees Fahrenheit can be maintained for about two hours. Such temperatures cannot be achieved and maintained in an open bomb crater with a can of gas. Gasoline poured on the open ground creates an impressive flash fire that lasts several seconds at most, not a high temperature fire lasting several hours.

It is hard to believe that Hitler would stay and take his own life while his entire staff enjoyed a safe escape.

In the illustrated World War II Encyclopedia, Volume 16, page 2174 we read: "In May 1945, Josef Stalin assured Harry L. Hopkins (personal advisor and emissary of President Franklin D. Roosevelt) that in his opinion Hitler was not dead and that he was hiding somewhere after escaping on a German U-boat."

On July 17, 1945, at the conference in Potsdam, Germany, a cablegram from the State Department in Washington was flashed to President Truman. It read:

"...The State Department is checking newspaper dispatches from South America, reporting rumors that Adolf Hitler and his wife, Eva, are in Patagonia."

Chapter 8

On March 24, 1945 the U-234 was moored at the Hindenburg harbor in Kiel, Germany. She was ready for departure. Her vertical mine-laying shafts contained ten steel cylinders, each lined with gold to shield crewmen from the 560 kilograms of enriched uranium inside each container—enough altogether for about a dozen nuclear bombs. In the revamped cargo hold was a crate containing infrared proximity fuses designed to detonate atomic bombs at pre-determined altitudes. In addition, there were boxes and suitcases containing plans, blueprints and other classified materials useful in manufacturing and using weapons of mass destruction.

Also on board were plans, products and supplies to help Japan bolster its mostly ineffective air defense systems on the Japanese mainland. Before the war in Europe ended, the German air defenses had managed to shoot down 8,325 American bombers. The Americans won only because they had more bombers than the Germans had artillery shells. In February, 1944, the Germans shot down 420 allied bombers in a single week.

On the other hand American bombers met little resistance over the Japanese mainland when they started dropping bombs in late 1944. Before the nuclear bombs were dropped, conventional American bombs destroyed sixty percent of the surface area of Japan's sixty largest cities, with the Americans losing only 414 planes in the process.

In addition to uranium and fuses for atom bombs, the U-234 carried a wide assortment of plans and materials, and also the personnel to help Japan strengthen its defenses.

Included in the cargo were two disassembled turbojet aircraft, the Messerschmitt 163 and 262, a pressurized cabin, fire control computers, Lorenz 7H2 bomb sites, and the latest German radar systems.

Passenger Erich Menzel was a radar and communications expert. Fritze von Sanraft was former head of anti-aircraft defenses at Bremen, Germany. In Japan their assignment was to update air defense systems and train technicians. Passengers August Bringewald and Franz Ruf were employees of the Messerschmidt aircraft company.

It was late afternoon when Kapitanleutnant Johann Fehler gave the order to start the engines.

Slowly, the giant submarine which was almost as long as a football field, moved away from the dock. Some people were waving as a brass band played the German national anthem.

On deck, officers and crew were lined up. On the bridge, Kapitanleutnant Fehler saluted back to well-wishers. Slowly, the giant submarine headed for the open sea.

Below deck, traveling with the cargo, was a special group of passengers. There were two Japanese officers, assigned by the Japanese government to oversee the shipment of this special cargo to their homeland. German scientists on board included Heinrich Hellendorn, Heinz Schlicke, Gerhard Falck,

August Bringewald, and Franz Ruf. Also on board was Nazi judge, Kay Nieschling, who Fehler described as follows:

> Our strangest "catch" was a naval judge, and the story of how he came to be with us is symbolic of the endurance of red tape, however severe the stresses of war.
>
> Some unscrupulous German merchants in Japan, making enormous profits from the nation's need for rubber, had been stupid enough to boast about their racket. News of their boasting had reached our naval attaché in Tokyo. Very properly worked up about it. This attaché succeeded—against some local opposition—in forcing through a report to Berlin, but once the officials got hold of it the argument dragged on and on interminably. First a court-martial was suggested; then it was discovered that we had nobody in Japan of sufficient rank to instruct the Court. Next, when there was talk of promoting someone to do the job, it was argued that the culprits were civilians. So it continued, and now, after months of wrangling had served to confuse the issue even further, it had been decided to despatch Captain-Judge Nieman to Japan in order to sort things out.
>
> The presence of the Judge was unfortunate, to say the least. A man of upright and honorable behavior, he was at the same time, quite devoted to the Nazi Party and Hitler. A thorough Nazi, though in the best, and therefore the most "inconvenient" sense of the word, he clashed violently with the General (C. Kessler).

Upon leaving the harbor at Kiel, the U-boat picked up speed, passing the narrow strait of Laboe-Friedrichsort at the Fieler Foerde. The ship then turned west to reach the Strande-

Bucht, a small fishing village on the shores of the Baltic Sea, where she anchored for the night. The big submarine maneuvered among some fishing boats to reduce the chance of being spotted by enemy aircraft, and there dropped anchor.

Fehler and his first mate, Karl Pfaff entered the village, looking for some good German beer, and a place to discuss their mission in private.

They knew the war in Europe was almost over, that Hitler's Third Reich would soon be history. Japan was their ally. America was the enemy. American planes had been dropping bombs on German military and civilian targets for nearly three years. Since the war in Europe was still raging, they probably did not discuss the pros and cons of abandoning their mission.

When the two officers returned to their ship that night, they were glad to be heading for the open sea because American bombers were lighting up the sky over Kiel with a night bombing attack.

It was 4:30 a.m. on March 25 when the U-234 raised its anchor and headed out to sea. Three escort vessels had arrived during the night, U-516, U-1107 and U-1274, all submarines, but smaller and slower. The convoy headed for Horten (Oslo Fjord), Norway. Fehler's log entry: *Marsch nach Horten durch den Grossen-Belt.*

The submarines traveled on the surface to avoid the many mines that infested these waters. After passing through the neutral waters of Denmark, the convoy hugged the Swedish coastline and headed for the Kategat which would take them toward Fredrikshaven, the northern port of Denmark. At noon on March 26 Fehler left the slower escort vessels behind because they could go only half the speed of the U-234.

The U-234 left Fredrikshaven in the night in order to cross the Kategat at full speed under cover of darkness. She arrived at the Horten U-boat base in Norway the next morning, the first and possibly most dangerous leg of the journey behind her.

The next stop was Christiansand on the southern coast of Norway. More passengers came on board: Colonel Fritz von Sandrath, First Lieutenant Erich Manzel and Air Force General Ulrich Kessler, who commanded the German Air Force in the north Atlantic, coordinating his war efforts closely with Admiral Doenitz, commander of the German Navy in the Atlantic. Kessler wore the Knight's Cross around his neck.

The names of the additional passengers were not listed in the log when they boarded the boat or when they left the ship near the Argentine coast. All we know is that, if they left the boat in Argentine waters, as described in the radio operator's log, they would have to have boarded the submarine at Kiel or one of the Norwegian ports.

There are no log entries for the U-234 from April 5 to April 15 while she was moored at Christiansand. Fehler describes the repairs as follows:

A terrible jar shook the boat from bows to stern; an "electric shock" that raced through the steel plates of the deck, then hurled us willy-nilly from our feet. Came a chorus of shouts...a screeching of breaking steel. Then the trim went haywire.

We had been hit by a sister U-boat; a U-boat that, turning carelessly from her own training area, had charged slap-happily into ours. She had carved into our "outerskin"; she had ripped open Number Seven tank, and she had let the sea water into the fuel. These facts we ascertained later (much later it seemed) when U-234 had regained the surface and we were free of the close confinement of her hull. But at the time it was as though we had been struck by a depth charge.

After we had told the other fellows what we thought of them, we inspected the damage. The jagged hole was at least twenty-four feet square, and thirty tons of our U-boat's precious fuel had been spewed into the sea.

Fortunately, the collision had occurred only a mile or so offshore, and the sea was calm, but when we entered the harbour and I asked our U-boat training officer to fix a dry dock, he told me that all were occupied. So the High Command intervened—and ordered us to Bergen, Norway.

None of us fancied the move, which would have entailed our limping along the Norwegian coast, an easy prey for the enemy aircraft, M.T.B.s and submarines that now made this area their hunting ground. So—as so often in her chequered past—U-234 used guile and craft to keep her out of trouble. To this day I am unable, for obvious reasons, to recount precisely how she "acquired" a suitable steel plate; suffice it to say that a satisfactory under-the-counter deal was negotiated and delivery effected by train from Oslo. Twenty-four hours later our submarine, having coyly declined her invitation to Bergen, had reached another anchorage and a self-help programme had begun...

First, we submerged her nose, flooding the forward tanks to raise the stern above the water. This was by no means an easy task—not with a submarine three hundred feet long. It necessitated giving the boat an

*inclination of about twenty degrees by the head, and
even then the lower rim of the hole was only one inch
above the surface, while the tide threatened to pour into
the conning tower hatch. Next, working parties blew off
the jagged edges of the hold, removed the bent and torn
frames, cut fresh ones from our acquired steel plate, and
welded the parts together with electricity generated by
U-234's engines. We had anchored near Christiansand,
where sea-bound U-boats had their last checkup before
sailing; and thus we managed to get oxygen from the
shore instead of having to use up our own most precious
stock. But we could only weld in the lower part of the
hole when the harbour was dead calm. Christiansand
could not spare us more than the daily help of one
workman, and the weather was often bad. Yet, despite
such difficulties, the job was finished within the week. A
real shipyard could have done no better!*

In addition to making needed repairs after a collision
with another German ship, she was waiting for additional
passengers and supplies.

We can only guess at who the unnamed passengers might
have been. Hitler and his wife are candidates. Some Nazi
leaders conspicuously missing at the Nuremberg trials
following the war included Adolf Hitler, Martin Bormann,
Adolf Eichmann, Dr. Mengele, Klaus Barbie, Friedrich
Schwend, Franz Paul Stangl, Rolf Guenther, and Herbert
Cukurs.

When the U-234 surrendered, U.S. military documents
list twelve non-crew passengers. In his book, *Dynamite for
Hire*, Fehler said his submarine was retooled to carry twenty-

six non-crew passengers (page 145). If we subtract the twelve who were accounted for at the time of surrender and the two Japanese officers who killed themselves, that leaves twelve available spaces. Neither Fehler, his officers, or passengers, ever named the twelve additional passengers, though Fehler said all available spaces were taken when the submarine left Norway. We know from the radio operator's log that after the war in Europe ended, but prior to the U-234's surrender, Fehler met another, smaller, submarine off the coast of Argentina, where unnamed passengers transferred to the smaller submarine. We can only speculate the identity of these unnamed passengers.

When the U-234 finally resumed her journey, April 15, she had a new escort, a U-Jaeger (PT boat) that could travel sixteen knots, almost as fast as the U-234.

At Lindesnes, on the southern tip of Norway, the escort vessel was left behind as the U-234 headed for the deep, safe waters of the Norwegian Trench. Fehler's last message to the skipper of the U-Jaeger: *"Gute Fahrt und gesunde Heimkehr"* (Have a good trip and safe return.)

Upon reaching the deep water, the alarm signal sounded and the U-234 submerged, on a new course of 320 degrees. Underwater her top speed was eight knots, as opposed to twenty on the surface, but she had orders to stay submerged until she reached the safer waters below the equator.

German submarines were equipped with an electric motor and two diesel engines for traveling on the surface, and a battery-powered electric motor for traveling underwater. On most submarines the diesel engines could not run beneath the surface because there was no source for intake air needed for combustion.

During the early years of the war, when in enemy territory, the German submarines would travel on the surface at night, allowing the diesel engines to recharge the batteries needed to travel underwater by electric power during the day when risk of being seen by enemy planes or ships was greatest. But as the war progressed and radar capabilities on allied ships and planes increased, it became increasingly dangerous for German subs to travel on the surface, even at night.

Toward the end of the war, an increasing number of German submarines were equipped with snorkels which enabled the ships to take in air for the diesel engines while traveling beneath the surface.

The U-234 was equipped with a snorkel, making it possible for her to cruise submerged all the way to the equator.

The U-234 traveled silently, no radio communication. The crew had not been told the destination was Japan, though some had probably surmised this because of the two Japanese officers on board.

At approximately sixty three degrees north, the ship turned west toward the Atlantic. The last obstacle before reaching open waters was the Rockall Rise, an area with sandbanks and shallow waters between Iceland and the Faeroe Islands.

Spirits were high among officers and crew. There was a feeling their mission would have some bearing on the outcome of the war.

When darkness fell, Fehler ordered the ship to the surface, temporarily, to reduce the risk of bumping one of the shallow sandbars. The hatch opened, allowing the skipper and some of the officers to step up on the bridge. A rough sea and low clouds hampered observation. Below deck the radio operator was watching and listening for any sign of approaching boats or aircraft. All was clear.

"*Aeusserste kraft voraus* (full speed ahead)," the skipper ordered. The engine room responded, the boat vibrated as she crashed through the large waves of the North Sea, soon reaching top speed of twenty knots. She was not only one of the largest U-boats in the German Navy, but one of the fastest as well.

Twice during the night, the alarm sounded, causing the U-234 to slip quietly beneath the surface to avoid observation from enemy aircraft. By daybreak she reached the open waters of the Atlantic. Her new course was south by south-east, under water again, at snorkel depth. Sometimes at night, she resurfaced in order to enjoy top speed.

The U-234 could average about thirteen knots, or about fifteen miles per hour. She could travel over three hundred miles in a twenty-four-hour period.

Each degree of latitude on the map is seventy miles, translating into the ability of the ship to cover over five degrees latitude each day. Using this calculation, she could easily have been below the equator on May 8, twenty one days after leaving Christiansand. This was the day Fehler received his last dispatch from Admiral Doenitz at Atlantic headquarters, announcing the war in Europe was over.

After ordering the boat to submerge, Fehler assembled the crew to make the announcement. The news was met with mixed feelings, relief that the fighting was over, but sadness that Germany had lost.

It is doubtful that this last communication from headquarters said anything about the surrender agreement requiring the U-234 to abandon her mission, because Fehler did not hesitate telling the officers and crew that their orders were to continue on their mission to Japan. Undoubtedly, the two Japanese officers on board were much relieved.

Hidio Tomonage and Oberst Shoji apparently had a working knowledge of the German language. They had been stationed in Berlin. In the close confines of submarine travel we must assume there was verbal interaction between the Japanese and German officers, especially at mealtime, but at other times too. There was nothing else to do.

The men certainly discussed the war, the Germans knowing more about the situation in Europe; the Japanese knowing more about the Pacific war. If the German officers attempted to shock their Japanese companions with horror stories of Hitler's treatment of the Jews, the Japanese could match them story for story with similar stories of Japanese atrocities in China.

After the meeting with the crew, Fehler invited Luftwaffe general Ulrich Kessler to his quarters where the skipper explained that he had orders to rendezvous that very night with another German submarine which was coming to pick up the twelve unnamed passengers. The rendezvous was supposed to take place at midnight.

Shortly before midnight, the U-234 returned to the surface and reduced her speed. She had reached the designated rendezvous location. With no moon, the night was dark. The sea was calm.

Fehler and his officers climbed onto the bridge, looking through their binoculars in an attempt to locate the approaching vessel. Below deck the unnamed passengers were preparing to leave.

Shortly after midnight the officers saw a light flashing in the distance. Kramer, the signal operator on the bridge asked if he should flash a response.

"No," Fehler responded. "Let's make sure she is the right one. We don't want to walk into a trap."

He watched the distant signal for a few more minutes before giving Kramer permission to respond.

A short time later the two boats met, in total darkness, pulling alongside each other.

The other vessel was probably the U-530, commanded by Kapitanleutnant Wermuth, who was operating in Argentine waters at the time, and surrendered in an Argentine port a short time later.

Without turning on any lights, twelve unnamed passengers quietly climbed from the U-234 to the U-530. There were some handshakes and words of appreciation as the guests departed.

Quietly, the two boats pushed apart, the U-530 headed west toward South America. The U-234 headed southeast toward the Cape of Good Hope (South Africa). Fehler retired to his quarters.

The details of the rendezvous were entered in the radio operator's log, but if Fehler wrote anything in his log, it was later destroyed.

We can only guess the things Fehler pondered that night. Looking at his iron cross, he certainly thought about his loyalty and commitment to his country. The war in Europe was over. He had orders to take his cargo and passengers to Japan. But Nazi leaders were abandoning ship, like rats.

If he completed his mission, Japan would have the materials and know-how to make atom bombs. How would the Japanese use such weapons?

We can be fairly certain that Johann Fehler didn't sleep that night, because the next morning he called his officers together for a special meeting. General Kessler, the highest ranking officer on board, also attended the meeting.

Fehler expressed his desire to abandon the mission to Japan and disappear somewhere in the South Pacific. Fehler made sure the men knew that in addition to 900 bottles of whiskey, the cargo included shotguns and rifles, fishing gear, an outboard motor for scouting inland rivers, mosquito netting for jungle camping, and fur-lined clothing, skis and snowshoes for climates closer to the South Pole.

Fehler was concerned that the scientists on board, some of whom were loyal Nazis, might protest. Certainly the two Japanese officers would be opposed.

We do not know how much time Fehler and his officers needed to make what might be argued the most important decision of World War II, only that they met twice, before announcing their final decision to the crew.

After a chat with Bulla and Pfaff, I decided that it would no longer be practicable, desirable, or, in view of the division of feeling among the company, justifiable, to pursue our lone voyage. My announcement to the crew was brief.

"Comrades," I said. "It is with great reluctance, after all your loyalty and obedience, that I tell you that it is now your duty as good soldiers to obey with me the orders of Grand Admiral Doenitz, and surrender to the Western Powers."

There was a deadly silence and then, as I gave the Stand Down, a low murmuring.

I climbed to the bridge. One of my most senior petty officers was standing there. He was staring stonily at the horizon, yet seeing nothing, for tears were running down his cheeks.

We don't know how many of the officers, if any, argued to continue the mission to Japan, but we do know that in the end they reached a consensus, though it was not what Fehler wanted.

General Kessler, who apparently knew a lot more about the cargo and its importance to the outcome of the war, wanted to surrender to the Americans. When Fehler said a surrender to the Americans was too dangerous, Kessler asked to be dropped off on the North Carolina coast to make his way inland where he would approach American authorities himself. When Fehler objected that it was too dangerous at this point in time to approach the U.S. coastline, Kessler asked to be dropped off in Argentina where he would contact American authorities at the U.S. Embassy.

Fehler was determined to find an uninhabited island. Kessler was determined to surrender to the Americans. The two officers argued through the night, but in the end Kessler won, and it was decided to surrender to the Americans.

It fell in Fehler's hands to tell the German scientists and the Japanese officers that the mission to Japan had been aborted, and that the U-234 was going to surrender to the Americans.

First, Fehler and Kessler approached the rest of the German military men and scientists. They did not ask the Nazis to vote on the issue, or to express opinions. They were merely told the decision had already been made, and all were expected to cooperate. If any disagreed with the decision, it was too late to do anything about it.

The Japanese officers were a different matter. When they expressed strong opposition to the decision, Fehler informed them he was not seeking input, nor was there an election in process. The decision had been made. All the ship's officers were in agreement. He was merely informing the Japanese officers that plans had changed. At the same time, Fehler disarmed the two officers, and ordered them confined to quarters, to prevent possible mutiny on the part of the Japanese.

Next, Fehler told the crew why the ship was now going full speed in the opposite direction.

Though the Japanese officers remained firm in their resolve to continue the mission to Japan, and used every argument they could think of to persuade Fehler to change his mind, Fehler would not bend. They even told him they would take no part in a surrender to their enemies, the Americans—that is was against their military code of honor. If the commander remained on this present course of action, the Japanese officers informed him that they would commit suicide by swallowing capsules of a drug called luminal.

"That is your choice," Fehler responded, coolly. "I will not force you to surrender to the Americans. Neither will I prevent you from swallowing poison." In his book, Fehler said he offered to drop off the Japanese at a neutral port before surrendering.

Resolved to their fate, the two officers asked Fehler to see that they were buried at sea after they died because they didn't want the Americans to have their bodies. The commander agreed.

I went aft and found the Japanese lying in their bunk...very still, their arms linked together; a luminal bottle, quite empty, lay tell-tale on the floor. We tried to revive them, but it was in vain. Attached to their pillow was a letter addressed to me. My hand shook as I opened it.

"Dear Kapitanleutnant," I read. "As Japanese officers and soldiers of the Emperor we are not permitted to fall alive into enemy hands. We know that you realize this, and we feel that a concern for our future may be embarrassing you in the decisions that you have to make."

The letter then made a polite reference to "our kindness" and concluded: "So, in case you find us alive here, will you please leave us alone and let us die."

For a moment the pathos of that last sentence almost overwhelmed me.

"Please leave us alone and let us die..."

And I had—even though it was by accident. For that message to the bridge had been delivered fully two hours earlier.

The simple dignity of the Japanese humbled us all. They seemed to have thought of everything, even to the extent of drafting a pathetic little will and testament assigning various treasured possessions to members of the crew who had been of service to them, or with whom they had worked. For me they left a sum of francs together with the request that I should use the money to inform their relatives that "We are dead, but have not disgraced ourselves in dying."

Both of the Japs were Buddhists, but I do not think they would have been displeased with the Christian burial we gave them. For our homage was sincere. In many ways these representatives of a "barbarian" race had been an example to us all. They had never complained about the humble tasks assigned to them: they had never traded upon their rank; and they had never, so far as I could see, quarreled with each other.

We covered them with the Rising Sun, the flag that was to have flown from our bridge upon U-234's triumphal arrival in Tokyo. But just before I read out the noble words of the Prayer Book, I ordered the sword of the Samurai to be brought from its place of honour in *my cabin. I knelt on the deck and bound it to the senior of the two men. I felt, somehow, that it was the sort of gesture they would have appreciated.*

The death of the Japanese affected me profoundly, and seemed to render more urgent the decision to which I had half-consciously been inclining during the preceding week.

One of the earliest signals intercepted from our former High Command had revealed considerable activity among the Navy in the Baltic. Surrender or no, it was obvious that our ships had still been operating, snatching tens of thousands of soldiers and civilians from the clutches of the Red Army, and bringing them back to British-controlled Hamburg and Kiel. I had also followed certain wireless traffic between our destroyers and the British command structure that had been set up in Denmark. I found the picture confusing, to say the least, and I felt that, despite the much-boosted solidarity of the eastern and western allies, events might force a situation where even Germans could again become important. I was also (to be frank) developing a feeling of loneliness for which I had not bargained; a feeling that a wireless, if anything, intensified. It was apparent that most of our comrades in the West had dutifully surrendered, and that only three or four other U-boats shared with U-234 the determination to disobey. I began to see fresh obstacles to my plan, both moral and practical. How far, for example, was one justified to avoid sharing with one's people the responsibilities of defeat? And would those responsibilities be as grave as we had once supposed?

Still cautious, knowing the Americans were still hunting for him, Fehler kept his crew on battle alert. Torpedoes were ready to fire, and all guns were loaded. Fehler fully intended to defend himself should his boat come under enemy attack.

On May 14, after the U-234 had been at sea for fifty-one days, Fehler decided to break silence and attempt radio contact with the outside world. His location was about five hundred miles south of New Foundland.

Fehler handed a message to the radio operator, with instructions to send it. It was an offer to surrender.

Almost immediately they received a message from Halifax, Canada, asking them to give their position, and to head west on a course of 320 degrees. The skipper had no intention of surrendering to the Canadians.

Then the radio operator suddenly received a second, much stronger signal, coming from a nearby vessel. It was the USS Sutton, an American destroyer, asking the submarine to give its position.

Fehler responded, agreeing to surrender. It was the evening of May 14 when the two boats met, both stopping a safe distance from the other, exerting caution on both sides, not wanting to be lured into an ambush.

The U.S. skipper couldn't believe the size of the German U-boat. The Sutton aimed its big guns at the submarine. Since it was almost dark, the American skipper decided to wait until morning to board it.

At daylight a group of heavily armed U.S. sailors and Marines tied their shuttle boat alongside the U-234, and climbed on the deck, asking to see the captain.

Kapitanleutnant Fehler, his officers and crew, were already on deck, standing in a straight line. Fehler asked the Americans for permission to retire the German war flag for the last time. Permission was granted. At attention, the German sailors saluted the German flag as it was lowered.

One of the U.S. soldiers secured the bridge hatch in an

open position, using a large chain and lock, a precaution that would prevent the German submarine from submerging in the event surrender negotiations collapsed. The U-234 was now in American hands.

After a few moments, the Americans awkwardly tried to figure out which German crewmen should remain on the sub as the Sutton accompanied it to an American port. The Americans didn't assume they could run the ship without assistance from some of the German crew members. After selections were made, the remainder of the crew and passengers were transferred to the Sutton, including Fehler.

The Sutton sent the following message to Naval headquarters:

REFERENCE (A) COMPLIED WITH U-BOAT 234. 1600 TON MINELAYER SUPPLY TYPE X-RAY BAKER. DEPARTED KRISTIANSAND 15 APRIL BOUND FOR JAPAN. 38 PRISONERS ABOARD HERE INCLUDE COMMANDING OFFICER JOHANN HEINRICH FEHLER AND SEVEN NAVAL OFFICERS. MAJOR GENERAL ULRICH KESSLER AND TWO LUFTWAFFE OFFICERS. ONE CIVIL ENGINEER. ANOTHER ILL ON SUB. TWO JAP OFFICERS HAD KILLED SELVES BEFORE SURRENDER, SUB HAS VALUABLE CARGO AND PLANS. USS FORSYTHE (PF102) ACCOMPANYING WITH 1500 MILE FUEL SUPPLY. 1530 GCT POSITION 46-33 N 45-20 W. PROCEEDING IN ACCORDANCE REFERENCE (B) SPEED 12. ETA 2000 GCT 19 MAY. SOME AVAILABILITY...

After this cable was received in Washington D.C., Admiral Jonas Ingram, commander of the Atlantic fleet, announced that while bound for Japan, the U-234 had surrendered. Ingram ordered two more U.S. destroyers, the USS Carter and the USS Muir, to join the USS Sutton.

Surrounded by three destroyers, the U-234 was escorted to American shores. It was 7:30 Saturday morning, May 19, when the German submarine and its three escorts were sighted a few miles beyond the Isles of Shoals outside Portsmouth Harbor, near Boston. Escorted by two Navy tugboats the U-234 proceeded into the harbor under its own power, finally mooring at the mouth of the Piscataqua River. Three other surrendered U-boats were already there, the U-805, 873, and 1228.

A coast guard cutter brought in the officers and crew of the U-234, including the military personnel and scientists.

Chapter 9

When Germany surrendered to the Russians on May 2, there was a sigh of relief among the leaders of the Manhattan Project. Germany was no longer in the nuclear bomb race. The Americans now believed they were the only serious player.

But their relief was short-lived. When the U-234 surrendered twelve days later, with her payload of nuclear bomb materials bound for Japan, it was apparent the Germans had been collaborating with the Japanese in nuclear weapons development. How close were the Japanese to using nuclear weapons? How dependent were they on help from the Germans? Were there other U-boats, in addition to the U-234, carrying nuclear weapons materials and know-how to Japan?

While Captain Fehler with his officers and crew were sent to prison camps, the scientists and military personnel were flown to Washington D.C. for interrogation. Dr. Heinz Schlicke ended up in Wendover, Utah, helping the Americans learn to use the German infrared proximity fuses.

In the book *Enola Gay*, by Max Witts and Gordon Thomas, the authors discuss the testing of proximity fuses at Utah's Wendover bombing range (page 112). We could find no mention of proximity fuses in Manhattan Project literature prior to this. It is safe to assume that prior to the arrival of the U-234, the Americans did not have proximity fuses.

The above reference mentions First Ordinance Squadron personnel waiting to see if the "...latest adjustments they had made to the bomb's proximity-fusing system would work," and if "...the fusing mechanism worked at its present height of two thousand feet." This is the same elevation at which atom bombs reached critical mass over Hiroshima and Nagasaki less than two months later. There would be no reason to test conventional weapons at a two-thousand-foot elevation. Conventional weapons would be ineffective that high above targets.

One of the worries to plague American scientists throughout the duration of the Manhattan Project was the production of enough enriched uranium (U-235) and plutonium (PU-239). There had to be enough for experimental explosions on American soil—at least one explosion—to make sure the bomb worked. There was also the risk of wasting uranium or plutonium in the event the first bombs dropped on enemy soil did not explode, or if the bombers were shot down by enemy fire. Military leaders didn't know how many Japanese targets needed to be hit before the Imperial Government agreed to unconditional surrender.

After the arrival of the U-234, the American plan was to nuke a Japanese city every four or five days until surrender. If the Japanese Government was stubborn, there was now enough uranium, thanks to the U-234, to bomb a dozen cities.

The arrival of the U-234 with 560 kilograms of enriched uranium removed all concerns about shortages. There was enough enriched uranium in the gold-lined cylinders from Germany for a dozen bombs.

At the time of this writing we don't know how much German uranium was used in the bombs dropped on Japan, though it seems very likely that the proximity fuses were used. The uranium itself can be traced only as far as the Manhattan Project's processing facility at Oak Ridge, Tennessee.

It seems apparent, however, that the German materials at least provided a generous reserve, allowing the Americans to move ahead with an experimental weapon that had been tested only once on a stationary tower. Thanks to Captain Fehler, and General Kessler the Americans knew that if the first, second or even third bomb dropped on Japan were duds, or if planes carrying bombs were shot down, there was plenty of German uranium and fuses to keep trying until something worked.

At 2:45 a.m., August 6, 1945 (Pacific time) the Enola Gay left Tinian airbase. Her belly was heavy with a five-ton uranium bomb called Little Boy.

Her target was Hiroshima, where she intended to release the bomb from an elevation of thirty-two thousand feet, with the bomb set to explode at two thousand feet.

Some of the Manhattan Project scientists had signed a petition not to use the bomb on populated targets, but that is exactly what the military intended to do. Some scientists thought that blowing off the top of Mt. Fuji, without the loss of human life would be enough to convince the Imperial Government to surrender. Military leaders didn't agree, believing as many Japanese people as possible had to see the impact. They also decided that if the unconditional surrender didn't come after bombing Hiroshima, then they would bomb Nagasaki, and more cities after that, one every four or five days until unconditional surrender was achieved.

Nobody knew how many people the bombs would kill.

One guess was that there would be about twenty thousand casualties with each blast.

At 8:15 a.m., the Enola Gay's bomb bay doors snapped open. At 8:16 a.m., American leaders no longer needed to worry whether or not the bomb would work. Little Boy reached critical mass at two thousand feet over Dr. Shimas' clinic in downtown Hiroshima.

A mushroom cloud burst to sixty thousand feet, twice as high as the one in the New Mexico desert. A firestorm flashed across the city. Everything that could burn, burst into flames. In a few seconds 144,600 people were dead and wounded.

The captain and his crew circled the giant mushroom, mumbling things like, "My God, what have we done?"

"Successful in all respects," was the message sent to the home base. The same message was immediately relayed to Generals Marshall and Groves in the United States. The Japanese government had finally received a portion of the U-234's cargo, though it was not as they expected.

A plutonium bomb was dropped over Nagasaki a few days later. The war was over. The Japanese surrendered, unconditionally.

Back in the United States, Johann Fehler, his officers and crew, vegetating in prison camps, were never thanked or recognized for the role they played in helping win the war in the Pacific.

After eighteen months of interrogation in several prison camps, Fehler was allowed to return to Germany where he reunited with his wife. Because there were no maritime jobs for ex-Nazi submarine captains, he obtained permission to leave the country, eventually ending up in a little village on the shores of the Red Sea. He spent the remainder of his life commanding a ten thousand-ton Arabian-registered merchant vessel on a Mediterranean-Red Sea run. He died in 1993, survived by his wife and three children. No one ever nominated him or Ulrich Kessler to receive the Nobel Peace Prize.

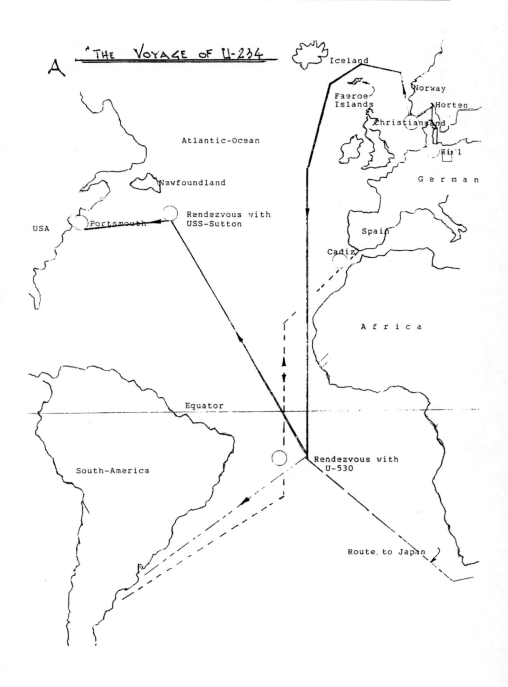

Exhibit 1

Johann Heinrich Fehler—Captain of the German submarine, U-234. This photo was taken about ten years after the 1945 voyage of the U-234. When the war in Europe ended, his plan was to abandon the mission to Japan and disappear into the South Pacific where he and his men could enjoy a relaxing vacation on a deserted desert island while the rest of the world sorted out the problems following the end of the war. He stashed sporting rifles, fishing poles and 900 bottles of whiskey in the hold to help with his plan.

Exhibit 2

Ulrich Kessler—General in the German air force who had fallen out of favor with the Third Reich and was being sent to Japan to help shore up Japanese defense against American bombers. Kessler refused to celebrate Hitler's birthday with Nazi shipmates aboard the U-234. When the war in Europe ended, it was Kessler, more than anyone else, who wanted to surrender the U-234's priceless cargo to the Americans.

Exhibit 3

Address reply to
Commandant,
First Naval District
and refer to
PRO-1/arc(0590)

HEADQUARTERS
FIRST NAVAL DISTRICT
NORTH STATION OFFICE BUILDING
150 CAUSEWAY STREET, BOSTON 14, MASS.

18 May 1945

MEMORANDUM FOR:

Captain Herbster
Deputy Commander Northern Group

Subj: Publicity on surrender of U-234.

At 1745 yesterday (Thursday, 17 May) I received from Captain George W. Campbell, Deputy Director of Public Relations, Navy Department, a telephone message stating that ComInch now authorizes me to permit press, radio and photographic coverage of the arrival of the U-234 at Portsmouth tomorrow morning with these two exceptions:

　　1. No press interviews with the prisoners will be permitted.

　　2. No press representatives will be permitted to go aboard the U-boat.

In response to questions, Captain Campbell stated that press and radio representatives and photographers may be taken in small craft to view and record the arrival of the U-boat at the buoy in Portsmouth Harbor, that photographs of this event may be taken but that it probably will be impracticable to arrange for photographs of the prisoners ashore. (Captain Campbell did not say such photographs were not to be permitted, providing circumstances made them feasible).

In short, Captain Campbell said we would handle the U-234 just as we have been handling press coverage of the preceding 3 U-boats, except that there will be no press interviews with the prisoners.

Lieut. Comdr. Allan Keller, PRO, 3 ND, informed me he had received similar instructions last night from Captain Campbell, who informed him that Admiral McCann would call Admiral Leary last night and confirm the instructions.

N. R. Collier,
Commander, USNR
District Public Relations Officer

Navy commander, N.R. Collier, prohibits press interviews with passengers on the German submarine, U-234. Press is not allowed on submarine, either. When three German subs surrendered earlier that week, press representatives were allowed to interview prisoners and tour submarines.

Exhibit 4

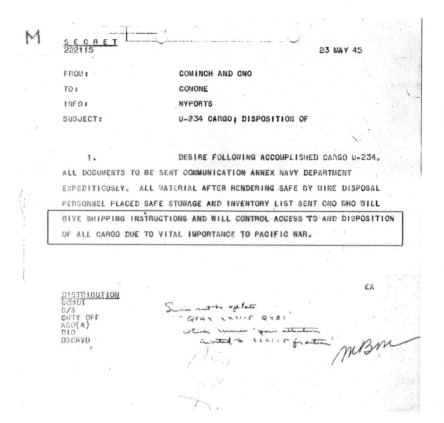

M

SECRET
222115   23 MAY 45

FROM: COMINCH AND CNO
TO: COMONE
INFO: NYPORTS
SUBJECT: U-234 CARGO; DISPOSITION OF

1.   DESIRE FOLLOWING ACCOMPLISHED CARGO U-234.
ALL DOCUMENTS TO BE SENT COMMUNICATION ANNEX NAVY DEPARTMENT
EXPEDITIOUSLY. ALL MATERIAL AFTER RENDERING SAFE BY MINE DISPOSAL
PERSONNEL PLACED SAFE STOWAGE AND INVENTORY LIST SENT CNO WHO WILL
GIVE SHIPPING INSTRUCTIONS AND WILL CONTROL ACCESS TO AND DISPOSITION
OF ALL CARGO DUE TO VITAL IMPORTANCE TO PACIFIC WAR.

DISTRIBUTION
COMDT
D/S
DUTY OFF
ADO(A)
DIO
DSCRVO

Naval telegram confirming importance of the U-234 cargo to
the war in the Pacific.

Exhibit 5

SECRET
262151 (P)

27 MAY

FROM: CNO
TO: NYPORT
INFO: COMONE
SUBJECT: MINE TUBES, UNLOADING OF

INTERROGATION LT PFAFF SECOND WATCH OFFICER U-234 DISCLOSES,
HE WAS IN CHARGE OF CARGO AND PERSONALLY SUPERVISED LOADING
ALL MINE TUBES.

PFAFF PREPARED MANIFEST LIST AND KNOWS KIND DOCUMENTS AND
CARGO IN EACH TUBE.

PFAFF STATES LONG CONTAINERS SHOULD BE UNPACKED IN HORIZONTAL
POSITION AND SHORT CONTAINERS IN VERTICAL POSITION.

URANIUM OXIDE LOADED IN GOLD LINED CYLINDERS AND AS LONG AS
CYLINDERS NOT OPENED CAN BE HANDLED LIKE CRUDE TNT.

THESE CONTAINERS SHOULD NOT BE OPENED AS SUBSTANCE WILL BECOME
SENSITIVE AND DANGEROUS.

PFAFF IS AVAILABLE AND WILLING TO AID UNLOADING IF RNEDT DESIRES.
ADVISE.

DISTRIBUTION
CONDT
C/S
DUTY OFF
ADO (A)
DIO
D ORD OFF

CTM

U.S. Naval communication confirming the presence of enriched
uranium (uranium oxide U-235) in gold-lined cylinders as part
of the U-234 cargo. (Please see letter on pages 41-43.)

Exhibit 6

25 MAY 1945

FROM: CNO
TO: NY PORTS
INFO: BUORD
        COMONE
SUBJECT: POW AND FUSES FROM U-234

LT (JG) H E MORGAN, LT (JG) F M ABBOTT, ENS F L GRANGER WITH DR SCHLICKE POW IN CUSTODY LEAVING ANACOSTIA NOON FRIDAY VIA PLANE. THIS PARTY EXPERT IN BOMB DISPOSAL AND PROXIMITY FUSES AND BEING SENT TO ASSIST IN SECURING CERTAIN INFRA RED PROXIMITY FUSES IMPORTANT BUORD AND IN CARGO U-234. FUSES WHEN SECURED TO BE RETURNED WASHINGTON CUSTODY ABOVE PARTY.

DISTRIBUTION:
COMDT
O/S
ACO
PIO (A)
BUERVO

D ONDOFF

DPRO

FJS

U.S. communication confirming the presence of infrared proximity fuses in the cargo of the U-234. These fuses, along with Dr. Schlicke, were routed to Wendover, Utah for testing, and eventual use in U.S.-made atomic bombs.

Exhibit 7

24 May 1945

MEMORANDUM

From: Jack H. Alberti.
To: Captain John L. Riheldaffer.

Subject: U-234.

The following information has been obtained from P/W Leutnant Menzel of the Luftwaffe, passenger on U-234.

1. The two after mine shafts of the forward line of six mine shafts amidships contain the personal baggage, documents and other property belonging to General Kessler, Oberst/Standart and Leutnant Menzel, in addition to some other cargo.

2. The Captain of U-234, Kapitänleutnant Fehler, and the II.W.O., Leutnant Pfaff (believed at Fort Meade), and the engineer of the boat (retained aboard U-234), between them, know most about cargo stowage and can be of great assistance in identifying it, as well as in proper and safe unloading.

3. In the U-Raum of U-234 there are two steel chests, marked Erich Menzel. These contain 15 rolls of secret films and all documents concerned with Menzel's mission.

4. U-843, C.O. Kapitänleutnant Herwartz, arrived in Norway from Japan about 10 April. She was sunk on her way to Kiel and two survivors were rescued by the Germans.

5. U-864, C.O. Kapitänleutnant Wolfram, was to go to Japan. She was sunk off Bergen with Japanese and German experts on board. Lt. Col. Stamp of the Luftwaffe and Obering Kahlfeldt, the high-frequency expert, who were to sail on this boat were not aboard and remained in Horten.

6. The packages for Dr. Schlicke, one of the passengers, and contained in one of the tubes are marked "TOMT". Dr. Schlicke knows about the infra-red proximity fuses which are in some of these packages. He warns that they must be handled with the utmost care as they may either explode or be irreparably damaged if handled improperly. Dr. Schlicke knows how to handle them and is willing to do so.

- 1 -

U.S. interrogation report with prisoner Erich Menzel, a Luftwaffe Lieutenant on the U-234. He mentions other German subs with business in Japan, secret documents and proximity fuses.

Exhibit 8

In reply address not the signer
of this letter, but Commandant, Navy
Yard, Portsmouth, N. H.

REFER TO NO.

U. S. NAVY YARD
Portsmouth, N. H.

162153   CR-986   17 MAY 1945

SECRET

FROM :   CNO

TO :   LT.CDR. HATTON

ARRANGE TO SEND ALL PASSENGERS X BELIEVED TO
BE TEN X FROM UNCLE DASH TWO THREE FOUR
DIRECT WASHINGTON BY NAVAL AIR X EITHER YOU
OR LT MAXWELL AND CAPT HERSHBERGER FROM COL
SWEETS OFFICE TO ACCOMPANY THEM X ADVISE
ETA DESPATCH X SEND OFFICERS AND CREW TO
HUNT IN USUAL MANNER BY PETER MIKE GEORGE X

SECRET

READDRESSED AS 170356
FROM: COMONE
TO : NYD PORTSMOUTH,NH

DISTRIBUTION:
A DE
CAPT OF YARD
LT. CDR HATTON .. ACTION

AUTHENTICATED BY:

F.H.HANBURY,LT.(JG)USNR

Secret U.S. Naval communication ordering transfer of U-234's
scientists and military personnel to Washington D.C.

Exhibit 9

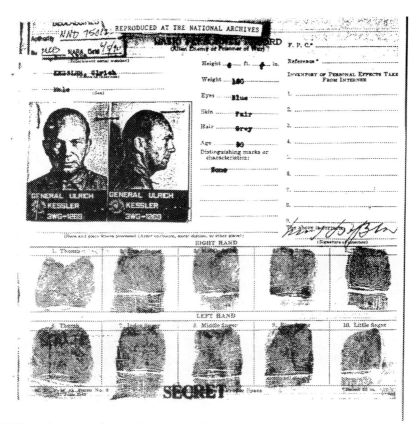

U.S. prisoner of war (POW) record for Major General Ulrich Kessler of the German Luftwaffe.

Exhibit 10

German submarine, U-234, in Portsmouth Harbor near Boston. Note the snorkel post in the center, a modification allowing the sub to run on diesel power while submerged.

Exhibit 11

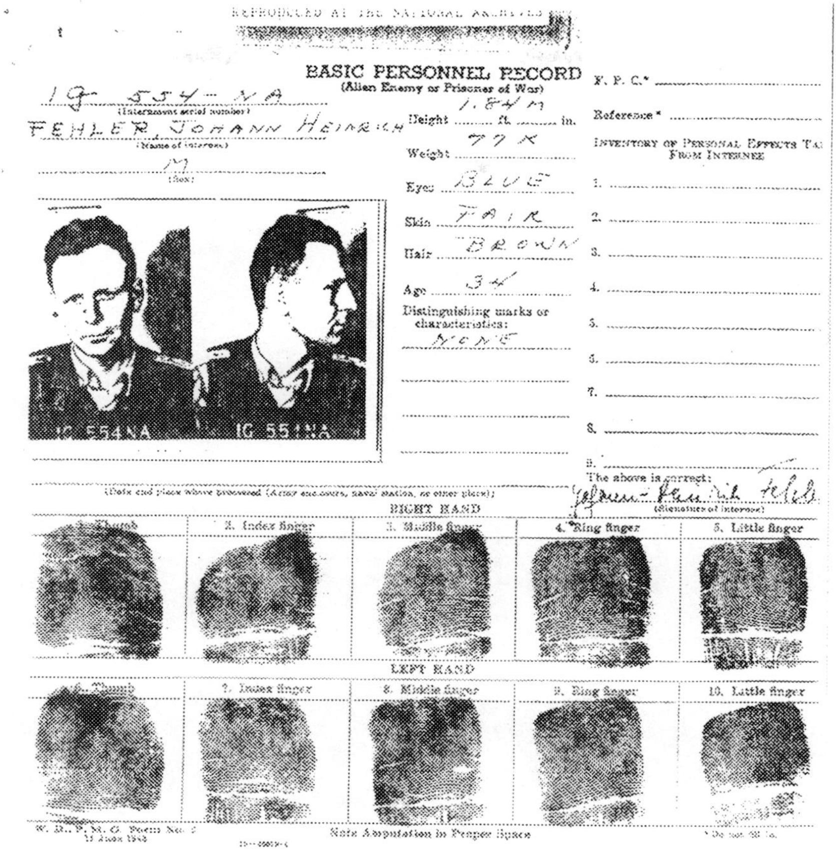

REPRODUCED AT THE NATIONAL ARCHIVES

BASIC PERSONNEL RECORD
(Alien Enemy or Prisoner of War)

1G 554 - NA
(Internment serial number)

FEHLER, JOHANN HEINRICH
(Name of internee)

M
(Sex)

Height 1.84 M ft. in.
Weight 77 K
Eyes BLUE
Skin FAIR
Hair BROWN
Age 34
Distinguishing marks or characteristics: NONE

F. P. C.*
Reference*
INVENTORY OF PERSONAL EFFECTS TAKEN FROM INTERNEE
1.
2.
3.
4.
5.
6.
7.
8.
9.

The above is correct:
Johann Heinrich Fehler
(Signature of internee)

IG 554NA IG 554NA

(Date and place where processed (Army enclosure, naval station, or other place))

RIGHT HAND

1. Thumb	2. Index finger	3. Middle finger	4. Ring finger	5. Little finger

LEFT HAND

6. Thumb	7. Index finger	8. Middle finger	9. Ring finger	10. Little finger

W. D., P. M. G. Form No. 1
Note Amputation in Proper Space

U.S. prisoner of war (POW) record for Johann Fehler.

Exhibit 12

U. S. NAVY YARD

PORTSMOUTH, N. H.

19 May 1945

From: Commandant, Navy Yard, Portsmouth
To: O.T.C. Surrender Unit, Northern Group, Eastern
               Sea Frontier

Subject: Prisoners, receipt for

1.   I have received from you this date delivery at Portsmouth Harbor of enemy submarine U-234 with _____O_____ officers and _seven (7)_ enlisted men retained on board U-234 by order of the officer in charge of the boarding party ComSubLant.

2.   I have also received from you this date delivery of the following _fifty nine (59)_ prisoners of war from the German U-234

     (a) 1 major general of the former Nazi Air Forces,
                      ULRICH KESSLER
     (b) _eight (8)_ additional individuals associated with the
              mission of said KESSLER
     (c) _six (6)_ officers of the U-234
     (d) _forty four (44)_ enlisted men of the U-234

Total 92 = 59

the above having been removed from the U-234 at sea to the USCGC ARGO, and landed at the Navy Yard, Portsmouth.

JOHN O. IVES
Lt. Cdr., USNR
By direction

U.S. Naval record showing dispersal of prisoners immediately after surrender.

Exhibit 13

COPY (MG)

USS SUTTON (DE-771)
c/o FLEET POST OFFICE
New York, N.Y.

15 May 1945

PASSENGERS AND CREW OF U-234

PASSENGERS

KESSLER, Ulrich		General der Flieger
X VON SANDRART, Fritz		Oberst
X MENZEL, Erich		Oberleutnant der waffe
X FALCK, Gerhard		Fregattenkapitan
KESSCHLING, KAY		Keschwaderrichter
X SCHLICKE, Heinz		Dr. Ing. Sonderfhrer Kervetten Kapt(MN)
X NELLENDORN, Heinrich		Oberleutenant Zur See
X RUF, Franz		Civilian

OFFICERS ON BOARD SUTTON

FEHLER, Johann Heinrich		Kapetanleutnant
PAGENSTECHER, Gunter		Oberleutnant Zur See
HIRSCHFELD, Wolfgang		Oberfunkmeister
WINKELMANN, Wilhelm		Obermaschinist

OFFICERS ON BOARD U-234

NULLA		Kapetanleutnant
ERNST		Kapentanleutnant (Ing)
WALTER		Mar. Stabsargt
PFAFF		Leutnant Zur See

CREW OF U-234 ON BOARD SUTTON

KINTZ, Wieland	UO 1193/38T	Masch Maat.
GERAUER, Rudi	UN 29049/475	FK Ob Gefr.
RAUHE, Herbert	UO 13863/43	Funk Gefr.
MAHIA, Adolf	UO 49239/42	Matr Ob Gefr.
DISTLER, Otto	UO 105/39T	Masch Ob Maat.
SCHNEIDER, Herbert	UN 9852/43	Matr Ob Gefr.
RAUSE, Herbert	UN 73838/43	Mech Gefr.
Starkensmeyer, Pulins	UN 6161/41	Masch Ob Gep.
SCHMINT, Helmut	13058/41	Matr Ob Gefr
ERNST, Steffen	UO 306/43	Masch Ob Gefr.
HOHN, Martin	UO 69805/42T	Masch Ob Gefr.
PAGEL, Kurt	UN 80981/41T	Masch Ob Gefr.
ERNST, Hans	UN 58872/42T	Masch Ob Gefr.
HAASE, Wilhelm	UO 11266/40T	Masch Hpt Gefr.
Vachmann, Werner	UN 3170/40T	Oberfunkmaat.
RUDOLPHI, Karl	UO 3881/39T	Maschinen Maat.
SCHNEIDER, Alfred	UO 9049/43T	Mat Ob Gefr.
HERMAIR, Peter	UN 3651/41KG	San Hpt Gefr.
WINTER, Lothar	UO 75589/42	Masch Ob Gefr.
LIEMANN, Georg	UN 410/40S	Ob Stem.
PUTZAS, Waldemar	UN 1093/40S	Matr. Hpt Gefr.
KIMMLING, Alfons	UO 7311/42	Masch Ob Gefr.
LEHMANN, Hubert	UO 42047/42T	Masch Ob Gefr.
HEINTEL, Karl	UNO 5535/41T	Masch Hpt. Gefr.
HUBER, Herbert	UN 12782/42	FK Ob Gefr.

List of all personnel aboard the U-234. The names marked with an X are the "German Scientists."

Exhibit 13 cont.

CREW REMAINING ON BOARD U-234

JASPER	Ob Strm.	NISCHE	Ob Strm.
SANDMULLER	Ob Masch.	SCHOLCH	BTsm.
THIES	Btsmt.	HUGGELE	Mech Mt.
KIATT	Masch Mt.	RICHTER	Masch Mt.
QUOSDORF	Masch Mt.	SIMON	Masch Mt.
SPUK	Matr Ob Gefr.	MOSTL	Matr Ob Gefr
SCHILLI	Matr Ob Gefr	GRUNTHALER	Mat Ob Gefr.
MEYER	Mech Ob Gefr	NOLL	Mech Ob Gefr.
SCHRAMM	Masch Ob Gefr.	WILIAN	Masch Ob Gefr.
WINTERMEYER	Masch Ob Gefr.	ENGELHARDT	Masch Ob Gefr.
KOPP	Masch Hpt Gefr.	WALTER	Masch Gefr.
WIEDENHOFT	Masch Gefr.	FUCHS	Matr Ob Gefr.

PASSENGERS ON BOARD U-234

✗ BRINGEWAID ✓   Civilian

USS ARGO
19 May, 1945

Received the above named prisoners, this date.

VICTOR D. HERBSTER
Captain, U.S.N.

Total from SE-& U 234 — 59
prisoners on U 234 — 07
Grand Total 66

94

Exhibit 14

Otto Hahn's model for splitting the atom, on display at the
Deutsche Museum in Munich, Germany.

Exhibit 15

$$\Delta E = E (1 - \cos \Theta) \frac{2M}{(M+1)^2} \qquad (3)$$

wo M die Masse des gestossenen Kerns in Einheiten der Neutronenmasse bedeutet. Der mittlere Energieverlust ist

$$\overline{\Delta E} = E \frac{2M}{(M+1)^2} \qquad (4)$$

Betrachten wir nun eine Anzahl n_0 Neutronen einer primären Energie E_0, so werden diese durch Bremsung Energie und durch Absorption und Spaltung an Zahl verlieren. Die zeitliche Energieverminderung ergibt sich in reinem Uran u zu

$$\frac{dE}{dt} = -E \cdot v \cdot \sigma_d \cdot c_u \cdot \frac{2M}{(M+1)^2} \qquad (5)$$

wo σ_d den Streuquerschnitt des Urankerns bedeutet. Die Verminderung der Zahl n erfolgt nach der Gleichung

$$\frac{dn}{dt} = - n \cdot v \cdot \sigma_s \cdot c_u \qquad (6)$$

wo σ_s der Wirkungsquerschnitt für die Kernspaltung des Urankerns ist. Dann wird

$$\frac{dn}{dE} = \frac{n}{E} \cdot \frac{\sigma_s}{\sigma_d} \cdot \frac{(M+1)^2}{2M} = \frac{n}{E} \cdot \gamma \qquad (7)$$

und die Wahrscheinlichkeit einer Unterschreitung der Schwellenenergie η

$$\eta = e^{\int_{E_s}^{E} \gamma(E) \, d(\ln E)}$$

Excerpts from a paper by nuclear physicist Fritz Hauterman of the Wilhelm Institute published in August, 1941.

Exhibit 15 cont.

Resonanz wird einfach

$$\ln w_r = - \int_0^\infty u \, d \ln E \qquad (18)$$

Setzt man für den Verlauf von $\sigma_{s,238}$ die Breit-Wigner-Formel ein, so ist es günstig zunächst von dieser einen zu 1/v proportionalen Anteil des Wirkungsquerschnittes für Energien, die hinreichend weit unter der Resonanzenergie liegen, abzuspalten. Die Ein-Niveauformel von Breit-Wigner für eine Resonanzeinfangung gibt:

$$\sigma_e = \sigma_0 \left(\frac{E_r}{E}\right)^{\frac{1}{2}} \left(\frac{\Gamma}{2}\right)^2 \left[(E-E_r)^2 + \left(\frac{\Gamma}{2}\right)^2\right]^{-1} \qquad (19)$$

und dieses zerlegen wir in einen Anteil

$$\sigma' = \sigma_0 \left(\frac{E_r}{E}\right)^{\frac{1}{2}} \left(\frac{\Gamma}{2}\right)^2 \left[E + \left(\frac{\Gamma}{2}\right)^2\right]^{-1} \qquad (20)$$

der erst bei thermischen Energien einen merklichen Beitrag zur Einfangung zeigt und den gleichen Gang mit 1/v aufweist, wie der Spaltungsquerschnitt, und einen eigentlichen Resonanzanteil

$$\sigma_{e,r} = \sigma_0 \left(\frac{E_r}{E}\right)^{\frac{1}{2}} \left(\frac{\Gamma}{2}\right)^2 \left\{\left[(E-E_r)^2 + \left(\frac{\Gamma}{2}\right)^2\right]^{-1} - \left[E_r^2 + \left(\frac{\Gamma}{2}\right)^2\right]^{-1}\right\} \qquad (21)$$

Dieser letzte Anteil lässt sich mit hinreichend guter Näherung für unsere Zwecke im Resonanzgebiet selbst, wo Ω (O) $\gg 1$ ist durch einen Ansatz der Form

$$\sigma_{s,r} \sim (E - E_r)^{-2} \qquad (22)$$

darstellen und wir erhalten

Exhibit 16

The completely assembled *Trinity* bomb in its tower shed, with physicist Norris Bradbury, July 15, 1945. Its detonation the next morning marked the beginning of the nuclear age.

Exhibit 17

The end of Berlin's secret runway used by Hanna Reitsch and other pilots during the final days of the war. Note the camouflage netting over the end of the runway to prevent enemy planes from spotting German aircraft. In the background is the Brandenburg Gate.

Exhibit 18

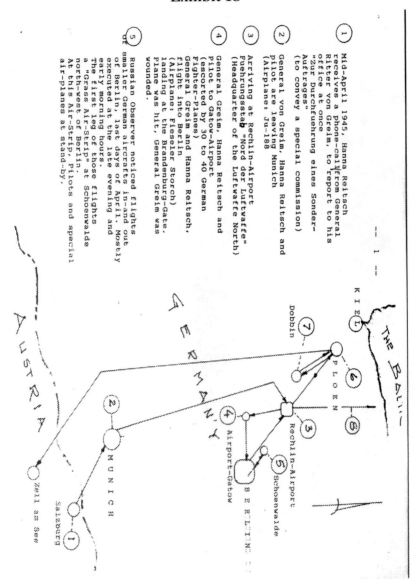

(1) Mid-April 1945, Hanna Reitsch receives a phone-call from General Ritter von Greim, to report to his office at once. "Zur Durchfuehrung eines Sonder-Auftrages" (to convey a special commission)

(2) General von Greim, Hanna Reitsch and pilot are leaving Munich (Airplane: Ju-188)

(3) Arriving at Rechlin-Airport Fuehrungsstab "Nord der Luftwaffe" (Headquarter of the Luftwaffe North)

(4) General Greim, Hanna Reitsch and Pilot to Gatow-Airport (escorted by 30 to 40 German Fighter-Planes) General Greim and Hanna Reitsch, flight into Berlin (Airplane: Fieseler Storch) landing at the Brandenburg-Gate. Plane was hit, General Greim was wounded.

(5) Russian Observer noticed flights of smaller German aircrafts in-and out of Berlin, last days of April. Mostly executed at the late evening and early morning hours. The first leg of those flights a "Grass Air-Strip" at Schoenwalde north-west of Berlin. At this Air-Strip, pilots and special air-planes at stand-by.

Flight path used by Hanna Reitsch and other pilots in and out of Berlin during the final days of the war.

Exhibit 18 cont.

(6) Generalfeldmarschal Ritter von Greim, the new Commander of the German-Luftwaffe; he and Hanna Reitsch are leaving Berlin; first landing at the Rechlin-Airport.
Hanna Reitsch insist to see Admiral Doenitz.
Flight to the City of Ploen (Headquarter of Doenitz)
Doenitz kept close contact with the German U-Boats Commander who are on stand-by, at Christiansand, Horten (Oslo), and Bergen, Norway.(Commander of the U-Boats North, FdU- Roesing.

(7) After she, Hanna Reitsch had the reassurance from Doenitz, she than had to see Field-marshal "Keitel", his headquarter was in Dobbin, a town only few miles north of the Rechlin-Airport.
After talking with Keitel, she flew back to Doenitz.
After the meeting with Doenitz, she had to meet with Fieldmarshal "Kesselring", who was at that time in Zell am See, Austria.
Commander von Greim and Hanna Reitsch arrived here May 8, 1945,
US-Forces took those fugitives in their custody......

Who was Hanna Reitsch?
She was the last of the "Hitlers" who convened personally messages from Berlin to Doenitz, from Doenitz to Keitel, from Keitel again to Doenitz, and from Doenitz to Kesselring, who wasn't anymore able to receive the message from Doenitz !
The new Commander of the Luftwaffe, Ritter von Greim had to follow the itinerary of this woman.
(Greim who was in great pain, wanted to go back to Salzburg)
These messages passed on by Hanna Reitsch so secret and so important they must have been, they never ever surfaced.
Hanna Reitsch was kept in US-Custody, xxxxxxxxxxxxxxxxxxxx" for 18 month.........
in "Solitary Confinement"

(8) From Rechlin-Airport (Stand-By Airplanes with special Pilots) to Stand-By U-Boats at Sea-Ports like Horten (Oslo-Fjord), Christiansand and Bergen, Norway.
Some well known German Pilots, we will find them later also in Argentina.
This was the "Northern Escape-Route".
Certainly there has been much more to this story, but Nazis kept their lips tied !!

Exhibit 19

Otto Hahn, the German chemist who received the Nobel prize in physics in 1944 for splitting the uranium atom, a discovery that was ultimately the basis for all methods to tap atomic energy, including the development of the atom bomb.

Exhibit 20

Captured officers and crew members of the German submarine
U-234 entering Portsmouth Harbor, May 19, 1945. Captain
Johann Heinrich Fehler in rear, nearest American flag.

Exhibit 21

German U-boat crew members enjoying a Saturday bath on a partially submerged submarine deck in the sunny Atlantic. The shortage of fresh water and stale air inside the submarine made outside bathing a refreshing change of pace.

Exhibit 22

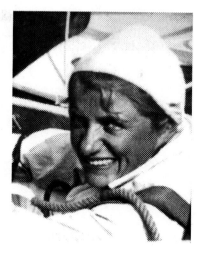

Hanna Reitsch—German test pilot involved in low elevation flights in and out of Berlin during the final days of
World War II. It is believed these flights enabled Nazi war
criminals, even Adolf Hitler, to escape capture by the
Russians.

Exhibit 23

SECRET
151745 (OP)   FOX 2471   15 MAY 1945

FROM: USS SUTTON (DE 771)

TO: COMINCH
               CINCLANT
               COMONE   (VIA RADIO WASHINGTON)

INFO: CTF 24
               CINCCNA
               FONF
               COMDESLANT
               CONTENTHFLT C&R
               ALL CTG'S OF TF 22
               COMSUBLANT

SUBJECT: U-BOAT 234; INFORMATION ON

REFERENCE: (A) ALLANT 20
               (B) USS SUTTON'S 150015

          REFERENCE (A) COMPLIED WITH ON U-BOAT 234.
1600 TON MINELAYER SUPPLY TYPE XRAY BAKER. DEPARTED KRISTIAN-
SAND 15 APRIL BOUND FOR JAPAN. 38 PRISONERS ABOARD HERE INCLUDE
COMMANDING OFFICER JOHANN HEINRICH FEHLER AND SEVEN NAVAL
OFFICERS. MAJOR GENERAL ULRICH KESSLER AND TWO LUFTWAFFE OFFICERS.
ONE CIVIL ENGINEER. ANOTHER ILL ON SUB. TWO JAP OFFICERS HAD KILL
ED SELVES BEFORE SURRENDER. SUB HAS VALUABLE CARGO OF PLANS.
USS FORSYTHE (PF 102) ACCOMPANYING WITH 1500 MILE FUEL SUPPLY.
1530 GCT POSITION 46-33 N 45-20 W. PROCEEDING IN ACCORDANCE
REFERENCE (B) SPEED12. ETA 2000 GCT 19 MAY. SOME AVAILABILITY.

REF (A)   PROCEDURE TO BE FOLLOWED BY SURRENDERING U-BOATS.
REF (B)   U-BOAT INTERCEPTION; INFORMATION ON

DISTRIBUTION
COMDT   PD
C/9   FAO   MPR   HM/JMD
DUIOFF   DPRO
(A) ACO DIO   DCGO
DSERVO

Secret U.S. document concerning the passengers and contents of the U-234.

Bibliography

Fehler, Johann, and A.V. Sellwood. *Dynamite for Hire: The Story of Hein Fehler*. London, Werner Laurie, 1956.

Hirschfeld, Wolfgang. *The Story of a U-Boat NCO, 1940-1946*. As told to Geofrey Brooks, Annapolis, Md. Naval Institute Press 1996.

Reitsch, Hanna. *Fliegen, Mein Leben*. Frankfurt, Ullstrin, 1988.

Scalia, Joseph Mark. *Germany's Last Mission to Japan: The Failed Voyage of U-324*. Annapolis, Naval Institute Press 2000.

Bundesarchiv-Militaerarchiv, Freiburg, Germany.

Portsmouth Naval Shipyard Museum, Kittery, Maine.

United States National Archives, College Park, Md.

United States National Archives, Waltham, Mass.

United States Navy Operational Archives, Washington, D.C.

About the Author

I, Arthur O. Naujoks, was born and raised in East Prussia in the city of Tilsit. (At this time the city is under Russian occupation and its name is now Sowjetsk.)

In 1941 I was drafted into the German army at age 18. After boot camp I was placed into an artillery-communication unit, where I was selected and trained as a forward observer. I didn't know at the time that this position was one of the most vulnerable, but I made it all the way through World War II.

The war in Europe ended May 8, 1945. I escaped from a POW camp, but I didn't have a home to return to. Most of Germany's citizens had fled to the west to be out of the reach of the Russians.

I finally found my family in the little town of Saxony, where I later met my sweetheart. We married in 1947.

My employment at the time was with the government in East Germany, since all industry and farmland was now under the ownership of the government. In the spring of 1950, I refused to become a member of the Communist Party, due to my religious beliefs. When I was six years old my family had joined the Mormon Church, and my beliefs made it impossible for me to join the Communist Party. I lost my employment and was told to report to a government agent to work as a slave-laborer in a uranium mine.

I realized the only way out was to pack a suitcase and try to reach West Berlin. My wife and I left behind all of our belongings, but by the next day we were in West Berlin.

We now had a new chapter of our lives in front of us. I soon found employment with Radio Free Europe.

At this time Berlin was well-known as a city where East and West could penetrate each other's lines. One day I was asked to meet a man who was a colonel in the U.S. Air Force. He asked me if I would be willing to help him make contacts with the East. I agreed to do so.

Finally in July 1953, my wife and I loaded up our few possessions and headed to the Rocky Mountains, settling in Salt Lake City, Utah.

My first job was at a Wonder Bread factory, where a foreman gave me a big broom and told me to start pushing it to clean the foor.

After a while we moved to California, where I found employment in the oil industry with The Texas Oil Company. I started in the labor-gang, at the grass-roots level.

My superiors liked my German work ethic and attitude, and it wasn't long before I was called in by the chief engineer. He asked me if I had some interest in working in the company's engineering department. I was certainly interested, and I agreed to take some evening classes in petroleum engineering at Long Beach College.

From that point on I worked on a permanent basis in their engineering department, and I did so until I retired from Chevron Oil in 1983.

With a comfortable pension, I began studying World War II history in earnest. I became fascinated with submarine warfare, and became curious with the refitting of submarines for hauling cargo and passengers to places like Japan. Digging a little deeper, I began finding bits and pieces of information concerning the mission of the U-234, and the efforts of the Germans to share nuclear technology with the Japanese.

My research experienced a major breakthrough in 1990 when the Freedom of Information Act was passed. Much of the information I sought suddenly became declassified.

I continued my research through the 1990s, eventually ending up with a file cabinet full of documents shedding light on Kapitanleutnant Fehler's historic voyage. In the year 2000 I teamed up with Utah writer Lee Nelson, who has helped me write this story of the Third Reich's last great secret.

In closing, I leave you this message: "He who reads, will never be alone."

Lee Nelson was born in Logan, Utah. He attended college in California and Utah, eventually earning a bachelor's degree in English and a master's degree in business (MBA). He has written 28 books, including the best-selling nine-volume *Storm Testament* series, and the *Beyond the Veil* series.

CEDAR FORT, INCORPORATED
Order Form

Name:_____

Address: _____

City: _____ State: _____ Zip: _____

Phone: (   ) _____ Daytime phone: (   ) _____

The Last Great Secret of the Third Reich

Quantity: _____ @ $19.95 each: _____

plus $3.49 shipping & handling for the first book: _____

(add 99¢ shipping for each additional book)

Utah residents add 6.25% for state sales tax: _____

TOTAL: _____

Bulk purchasing, shipping and handling quotes available upon request.

Please make check or money order payable to:

Cedar Fort, Incorporated.

Mail this form and payment to:

Cedar Fort, Inc.

925 North Main St.

Springville, UT 84663

You can also order on our website **www.cedarfort.com**

or e-mail us at sales@cedarfort.com or call 1-800-SKYBOOK